Strategies for Sustainability

Asia

IUCN: The World Conservation Union

Founded in 1948, The World Conservation Union brings together states, government agencies and a diverse range of non-governmental organizations in a unique world partnership. IUCN has over 800 members in all, spread across some 125 countries.

As a Union, IUCN seeks to influence, encourage and assist societies throughout the world to conserve the integrity and diversity of nature and ensure that any use of natural resources is equitable and ecologically sustainable. A central Secretariat coordinates the IUCN programme and serves the Union membership, representing their views on the world stage and providing them with the strategies, services, scientific knowledge and technical support they need to achieve their goals. Through its six commissions, IUCN draws together over 6000 expert volunteers in project teams and action groups, focusing in particular on species and biodiversity conservation and management of habitats and natural resources. The Union has helped many countries prepare National Conservation Strategies and demonstrates the application of its knowledge through the field projects it supervises. Operations are increasingly decentralized and are carried forward by an expanding network of regional and national offices, located principally in developing countries.

IUCN builds on the strength of its members, networks and partners to enhance their capacity and support global alliances to safeguard natural resources at local, regional and international levels.

The Strategies for Sustainability Programme of IUCN

Based on the principles of the World Conservation Strategy and *Caring for the Earth* [1], IUCN supports the preparation and implementation of strategies for sustainability in response to requests from governments, communities and NGOs. The Strategies for Sustainability Programme of the IUCN Secretariat and the Working Group on Strategies of the IUCN Commission on Environmental Strategy and Planning (CESP) assist those involved in strategies through a programme aimed at:

- undertaking conceptual development and exchange and analysis of experience concerning strategies throughout the world;
- carrying out demonstration and testing of key elements, tools and methodologies in strategies;
- building regional networks of strategy practitioners; and
- strengthening local capacity by engaging the networks in conceptual development, exchange and analysis of experience, and demonstration activities.

The programme draws on experience with all types of strategies regardless of their sources of support. Working group members include practitioners in national conservation strategies, national environmental action plans, other national strategies, international strategies, and a wide range of provincial (state) and local strategies.

1. IUCN, UNEP and WWF (1991). *Caring for the Earth: A Strategy for Sustainable Living.* Earthscan Publications, London.

Strategies for Sustainability

Asia

Jeremy Carew-Reid, Editor

IUCN Programme on Strategies for Sustainability

The World Conservation Union

Earthscan Publications Ltd.

Strategies for Sustainability: Asia was made possible by the generous support of the Swedish International Development Authority, the International Development Resource Centre (IDRC) and the Swiss Agency for Development Cooperation (SDC)

First published in the UK in 1997 by:
Earthscan Publications Limited, in association with IUCN

A catalogue record for this book is available from the British Library

ISBN: 1 85383 269 3

Design: Patricia Halladay

Earthscan Publications Limited, 120 Pentonville Road, London, N1 9JN, UK
Tel: 0171 278 0433   Fax: 0171 278 1142
Email: earthinfo@earthscan.co.uk
Web Site: http://www.earthscan.co.uk

IUCN Publications Services Unit, 219c Huntingdon Road, Cambridge, CB3 0DL, UK
IUCN Communications Division, Rue Mauverney 28, CH-1196 Gland, Switzerland

The views of the authors expressed in this book, and the presentation of the material, do not imply the expression of any opinion whatsoever on the part of IUCN concerning the legal status of any country, territory or area of its authorities, or concerning the delimitation of its frontiers or boundaries.

Printed and bound in the UK by Biddles Ltd, Guildford and King's Lynn

Printed on acid and elemental chlorine free paper, sourced from sustainably managed forests and processed according to an environmentally responsible manufacturing system.

Contents

Preface

This publication is part of an IUCN series of Regional Reviews of Strategies for Sustainability covering Asia, Africa and Latin America. The series is devoted to an analysis of lessons learned in multi-sectoral strategies at national, provincial and local levels. It is a joint effort by the Strategies for Sustainability Programme of the World Conservation Union (IUCN) and its Commission on Environmental Strategy and Planning (CESP). It was carried out in cooperation with other organizations such as the World Bank, The United Nations Development Programme (UNDP), The International Institute for Environment and Development (IIED) and The World Resources Institute (WRI) to assemble and analyze experience with strategies, and use this information to improve future strategy development and implementation.

Each volume consists of a status report that summarizes the status of strategies in the region, a synthesis of case studies, and individual case studies of selected strategies. The review attempts to cover only a sample of the region's strategies, recognizing that reviews such as this can never capture all the experiences that a region has to offer. The information presented here is up to date at the time the case studies were compiled (July 1993 - March 1995).

The case studies are not intended to be evaluations. They are analytical histories of strategies, providing a summary of basic information and lessons learned that has not before been readily available.

The case studies in this volume were prepared by members of the IUCN/CESP Working Group of Strategies for Sustainability in Asia, including individuals who have been closely involved in the development and implementation of the strategies, and who are from the country concerned. They were reviewed at a Workshop at Air Keroh, Melaka, Malaysia in November 1992.

It is important to emphasize that much of the field work undertaken in these cases are pioneering efforts in strategic planning and implementation. The educational value of the workshop was increased by participants' willingness to discuss their experiences frankly and openly. They focused on problems they encountered and lessons they had learned; and they considered their failures as good learning opportunities. Because of their openness and ability to reflect on their experience, the learning value of the workshops and case studies was increased significantly.

We hope these experiences provide valuable information, stimulation and motivation to others facing similar challenges elsewhere. The views presented in the case studies do not necessarily reflect those of the government agencies or the officials involved.

Acknowledgements

IUCN wishes to thank the authors of the case studies and the workshop participants for giving so freely of their time and experience in order to share with others the lessons they have learned through perseverance, trial and error. They are: Ishak bin Ariffin, Dulce M Cacha, Geoffrey Davidson, Aban Marker Kabraji, Ram Kadkar, G M Kattak, John McEachern, Syed Ayub Qutub, M S Ranatunga, Haroun Er Rashid, L Wijesinghe, Ranjit A Wijewansa. They were supported by a resource team fielded by the IUCN Strategies for Sustainability Programme, including: Jeremy Carew-Reid, Nancy MacPherson, Robert Prescott-Allen and Adrian Wood.

We are also grateful for the financial support from the Swedish Development Authority that enabled us to organize and host the workshop at which these case studies were discussed and analyzed, and finally, for the funds to publish and distribute this volume provided by the Swiss Agency for Development Cooperation (SDC). Local arrangements for the Air Keroh Workshop were made by WWF Malaysia. To these organizations, we offer our thanks for their support.

Nancy MacPherson
Coordinator
Strategies for Sustainability Programme
IUCN HQ, Gland, Switzerland

Information for the chapter title pages was taken from the following publications: *Rapport Mondial Sur le Développement Humain, 1993*. Economica, Paris, 1993; *World Development Report, 1993: Investing in Health: World development indicators*. The World Bank, Washington, DC, 1993; and *The Cambridge Encyclopaedia*, David Crystal (ed.), Cambridge University Press, Cambridge, Massachusetts, 1992. In some instances, additional information was also taken from *The New Encyclopaedia Brittanica: Micropaedia*, Chicago, Illinois, 1992.

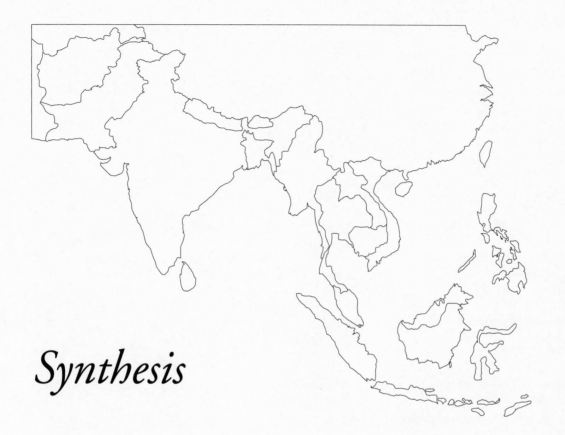

Synthesis

1 Overview

This volume presents a decade of experience with strategies for sustainability in six Asian countries, four in South Asia and two in Southeast Asia.

- Bangladesh: National Conservation Strategy and National Environmental Management Action Plans.
- Malaysia: National Conservation Strategy, nine state conservation strategies, and a conservation strategy for the federal territory.
- Nepal: National Conservation Strategy.
- Pakistan: National Conservation Strategy.
- Philippines: National Conservation Strategy, Strategy for Sustainable Development, and Agenda 21.
- Sri Lanka: National Conservation Strategy and Draft Action Plan, Environmental Action Plan, and National Environmental Action Plan.

The case studies include a diverse range of approaches to development and implementation, from strategies led by technical consultants, to those produced solely by government, to more participatory processes. Most follow the linear model, with production of a strategy document followed by implementation. However, there are a number of important innovations, such as the Environmental Core Group developed in Nepal and the Journalist Resource Centre for the Environment in Pakistan.

2 Relationship to Development Planning

Economic development, or the lack of it, has a bigger impact on the environment than environmental actions per se. To be fully effective, therefore, environmental strategies must exert a strong influence on development. They are most likely to do this if they are an integral part of development planning and policy making.

The national conservation strategies of Bangladesh and Sri Lanka were developed in parallel to development planning, without any tangible links to the development planning systems of either country. As a result, their success has been limited. In Bangladesh, for example, the strategy became marginalized within government, largely as a result of placing the strategy in an institution that was specialized and well outside the main economic and development machinery of government.

The strategies of Malaysia, Nepal, Pakistan and the Philippines are one step closer to achieving integration with development planning. These strategies have resulted in environmental and sustainability components being included in development plans, sectoral master plans, corporate strategies and programmes in each country. Although none combine development planning with the conservation/environment strategy, they do establish

5

some form of ongoing link with the development planning process. This has given them credibility within key economic and planning agencies; as a result, they have succeeded in influencing major policies and plans.

The national conservation strategy and many of the state strategies undertaken by Malaysia were planned in close collaboration with the economic planning unit in the Prime Minister's office, and the economic planning units in the states. Similarly, the Nepal National Conservation Strategy (NCS) was developed and is being implemented under the umbrella of the National Planning Commission.

In Pakistan and the Philippines, the links with development and economic planning institutions were not formalized or well-internalized. This has meant a delay between completion of the strategy and its formal integration into the work of development planning agencies. Although the Pakistan NCS had established close links with the chair of the planning commission, the strategy was not part of the working level of the commission or other key government agencies. Pakistan is now developing a formal link with the commission, in the form of an environment unit, to help implement the NCS. In the Philippines, while the Philippine Strategy for Sustainable Development (PSSD) and Philippine

Agenda 21 are explicitly tied in to the development planning system through the National Economic Development Authority (NEDA), the delegation of responsibility to a sectoral unit of NEDA casts doubt on whether the arrangement will be effective.

3 Conditions Needed

Conditions for an effective strategy include:

- a clear view of the strategy as the best way to tackle the issues concerned;
- wide understanding of the concept of a strategy and recognition that one is needed. Also required is a clear idea of the purpose of the strategy, its goals and objectives, and a feedback mechanism so it does not get off track. The objectives have to be those of the people implementing the strategy, and so must be set in a participatory manner;
- high-level political support for the development of a strategy, based on a clear understanding of what the process entails and its expected results;
- financial resources, either from government revenue, other participants, donor funding, or a combination of these;
- human and organizational resources for the development of the strategy;

- organizational arrangements to guarantee a certain level of administrative autonomy and independence, allow for cross-sectoral coordination, and enable the strategy to make an impact;
- a body of people committed to developing and implementing the strategy;
- a location for the body responsible for developing the strategy and coordinating its implementation where it can have the greatest influence on the national development system;
- adequate time to develop a strategy and a flexible schedule; and
- a good design.

Case studies confirm the necessity of obtaining support from key high-ranking government and political officials for strategy development and implementation. The Pakistan and Nepal NCSs are good examples of the benefits of this support. Through strategically nurtured support from high-ranking government and political officials, the Pakistan NCS survived three changes of government, while the Nepal NCS survived four changes; both strategies were successfully approved by cabinet. In Nepal, consistent support from the Prime Minister, the King, and a task force of high-level officials gave the strategy the support it needed to get through to endorsement and implementation.

In contrast, the high-level task force appointed to oversee the Bangladesh NCS failed to meet, and the opportunity to nurture high level support for the strategy was lost. As a result, neither the Bangladesh NCS nor the National Environment Management Action Plans (NEMAPs) have been approved by cabinet.

The Nepal NCS illustrates the benefits of activities that maintain public and political support throughout the strategy process. Nepal adopted a participatory approach to the NCS process by involving land users, village and district government institutions, private sector individuals and government officials in NCS formulation and demonstration projects.

Also, an Environment Core Group of more than 70 individuals was formed as the primary mechanism for policy development and capacity-building. The group, which draws technical experts from all key government sectors, has taken the lead in key institutional and administrative reforms. It represents an ongoing expert support base for further strategy activities.

The evolution of ten state conservation strategies and the national conservation strategy in Malaysia illustrate the importance of government's sense of ownership of the strategy, and the resulting motivation for implementing

7

actions. Some of the early state strategies disappeared from sight because they had been completed outside government by WWF-Malaysia and officials did not know what to do with them. Later state strategies broadened in scope and involved WWF working more closely with state officials. This approach has had a positive effect.

4 Internalizing the Strategy

Insufficient internalization of strategies, lack of government commitment and loss of continuity and momentum are common problems.

Nepal has achieved the greatest degree of internalization within government and development planning among the cases studied. A solid working relationship between the National Planning Commission (NPC) and sectoral ministries has been built up over the eight years of the strategy process. Technical capacity has increased and, under the guidance of the NPC, the Nepal NCS has made significant contributions to the fields of Environmental Impact Assessment (EIA), pollution control, environmental law, environmental planning, heritage conservation and environmental education.

The establishment of Environment Protection Councils in 1993, with the NPC as secretariat, was an important institutional initiative. Yet, without greater commitment by government to increased staff resources, the effectiveness of the councils will remain in doubt.

The PSSD has achieved some degree of internalization through its incorporation into the master plan of the Department of Agriculture, and its adoption as the corporate strategic plan of the Department of Environment and Natural Resources. It is currently intended to be integrated into the Philippine Medium-Term Development Plans (1993–1990). However, the institutional arrangements for this are weak.

While the Pakistan strategy document is thought to be one of the most comprehensive to date, internalization of the strategy within government is not far advanced. The Pakistan NCS has been driven and inspired for eight years from outside of government by IUCN-Pakistan. With top level government and political support, the NCS has successfully been adopted in Pakistan as the environmental agenda. However, the ongoing involvement of working-level federal and provincial government staff and resource managers in the strategy has been minimal. The current NCS implementation phase is beginning to tackle how best to internalize the strategy within the working levels of government to ensure that it is fully implemented.

The early Malaysian state strategies were not internalized by government because they were completed by WWF, which acted as a consultant to the state governments. The later strategies have achieved some degree of internalization because they were more closely developed with key state officials and economic agencies. Three strategies are in the implementation stage. A focus on resource economics in the national conservation strategy is providing valuable information to government decision-makers faced with tough choices related to export of tropical woods and protection of forests.

There has been little internalization of the Bangladesh NCS or NEMAPs. Neither has been formally approved by cabinet, and, lacking resources for implementation, there is a danger that both strategies will be overshadowed by other major initiatives, such as the Flood Action Plan.

5 Role of External Support

In Sri Lanka, five environmental strategy documents were prepared from 1982 to 1991. This seems partly a result of a preoccupation with documents rather than implementation. Poor coordination by donors also appears to have been a factor. This is a concern given the National Environmental Action Plan's reliance on donor support for implementation.

Other countries like Pakistan and Nepal have managed to stick to one major strategy initiative (an NCS), and not be sidetracked by other external demands. Both countries have insisted that the requirements of agencies such as the World Bank, United Nations Commision on Environment and Development (UNCED) and Agenda 21 must fit in with current initiatives. Pakistan regards the NCS as meeting the World Bank requirements for a National Environmental Action Plan (NEAP), and has declined to undertake expensive duplication of these efforts. The Bank has accepted the NCS as the NEAP with the exception of priority-setting for the Bank's requirement of an Environmental Investment Programme. In Nepal, an NEAP is being prepared within the framework of the NCS.

Several of the strategies indicate that a diversification of donor support for strategy development is desirable. Reliance on one donor can ultimately weaken the strategy since it is likely that most donors will not maintain long-term support for all its components. When a donor reduces support, key components of a strategy may be at risk. This is of special concern once implementation begins. The NCS team in Pakistan realized that the base of support had to be broadened when it became apparent that their major donor, CIDA, was no longer interested in supporting a broad range of strategy activities.

9

Bangladesh relied solely on the Norwegian Agency for International Development (NORAD) for support during strategy preparation. In retrospect, bringing in more donors would have increased understanding of the strategy and improved its chances of implementation. The Bangladesh example also illustrates the need for external backers, once involved, to maintain consistent support throughout the strategy development process and well into implementation. IUCN's inability to continue its support for the NCS has left participants feeling somewhat abandoned.

Although the Philippines SSD was prepared quickly and efficiently, donors and lenders have used it simply as evidence that a framework document has been adopted and a condition has been met. They have not used it as a framework for shaping and coordinating their support. This suggests the need to root the strategy more deeply in government and in the international donor community through greater participation of the former and thorough briefing of the latter.

The recent donors' conference for NCS implementation in Pakistan made it clear that the donor community, although generally supportive of the NCS, was uncertain how to get from the document to selected support for the 14 core programmes set out in the NCS. This illustrates clearly the need to work closely with the donor community and governments in setting out realistic steps to lead them from the current problems to the recommended solutions within the strategy. It should not be taken for granted that donors or governments will reach these solutions on their own.

6 Extent of Participation

The case studies make clear the value of broad-based involvement in strategy preparation to strengthen support, develop a deeper understanding of the issues, and build capacity within key agencies and communities to carry on implementation. At the inception of the strategies, most strategy staff from the various countries had a limited understanding of the real difference between consultation and participation and of the long-term benefits of the strategy process. They also didn't understand the skills and resources that would be required to carry out a truly participatory process, involving people on a substantive ongoing basis.

Of the cases studied, the Nepal NCS is the only strategy to achieve a significant degree of true participation. This has focused primarily on government through the work of the Environmental Core Group, involving people from key agencies and ministries in strategic environmental planning and environmental assessment exercises. In the community at large there were participatory processes of environmental assessment and planning with villagers and the private sector.

Many strategies have included various types of consultation, in the form of workshops, national conferences and public meetings. In some cases this consultation has involved large numbers of people; in Pakistan, for example, some 3000 people took part in the series of meetings during the NCS formulation phase.

Similarly, consultation for the Philippines SSD involved a national workshop and a series of multi-sector workshops and regional consultations. Participation in the strategies of Sri Lanka and Bangladesh was limited to consultation with key officials and NGO representatives in workshops during strategy preparation.

Most of the Malaysian state strategies had even less participation, since WWF-Malaysia prepared the strategy documents as consultants to government, and much of the work was regarded as confidential. The Malaysia NCS process is a more consultative one, however, involving universities, governments and the private sector.

7 Implementation

The Nepal NCS is the most advanced of the strategies in terms of implementation. One reason for this is the deliberate design of a very focused implementation strategy, initially concerned more with key environmental management methods and processes than substantive sectoral issues. Also, it has placed emphasis on demonstrating and developing the policy context and capacities which encourage actions by government and NGOs. This 'show the way by doing' approach, combined with a highly participatory style of involving government officials and communities in carrying out such initiatives as EIAs, land use and village plans, resulted in the development of five major programme areas: environmental assessment, environmental planning, heritage conservation, environmental education, and public information.

A unique aspect of implementing the Pakistan NCS is its communications programme. Creating a Journalist Resource Centre for the Environment at the inception of the strategy process provided an ongoing communications and publications facility for the NCS. Work is now being done for further implementation, including major support to government institutions and capacity-building within government, the private sector and NGOs.

The Bangladesh and Sri Lankan strategies illustrate the difficulties in implementation when the strategies have not been closely tied to key development planning agencies. There has been no implementation of the Bangladesh NCS or NEMAPs, and participants are discouraged with the lack of progress and the apparent duplication of effort by parallel exercises. In Sri Lanka, many years have been devoted to the preparation of strategy documents without commensurate result.

The Philippines SSD has been incorporated into the master plan for the Ministry of Agriculture, and has been used to justify many projects and programmes funded by donors and international

organizations. Otherwise, it has not been implemented.

The chequered progress of even the most successful strategies reviewed here demonstrate the need for monitoring and evaluation, including the definition of indicators for successful strategy development and implementation. The Pakistan NCS is the only strategy in the review to have had a monitoring process from its inception. Initiated as a requirement of CIDA support for the strategy, the monitoring process has provided course-correcting for the strategy, critical feedback to the donor, and the introduction of a participatory review process as a tool for evaluation.

Chart A: Status of Selected Strategies for Sustainability in Asia

Strategy	Status							Strategy Type
	A	B	C	D	E	F	G	
National								
Bangladesh				•				NCS, NEMAP
Bhutan		•						NES
China								NCS
India			•					NCS
Indonesia								
Laos						•		NCS
Malaysia			•					NCS
Myanmar						•		NCS
Nepal	•		•					NCS
Pakistan	•		•					NCS
Philippines	•		•					NCS, NSSD, NA
Sri Lanka			•					NCS, DAP, EAP, NEAP
Thailand								
Vietnam	•		•					NCS, NEAP
Regional/local								
Taiwan								CS
Malaysia:								
Kedah				•				SCS
Kelantan	•		•					SCS
Kuala Lumpur	•		•					FCCS
Melaka				•				SCS
Negeri Sembilan								SCS
Perlis	•		•					SCS
Sabah	•		•					SCS
Sarawak			•					SCS
Selangor	•		•					SCS
Trengganu				•				SCS

A   Main implementation phase.
B   Implementation concurrent with initial development.
C   Formal adoption of strategy document by the appropriate authority.
D   Initial development phase completed; strategy docu–ment awaiting approval; little or no implementation.
E   Initial development phase, primarily information assembly and analysis, policy formulation, action planning.
F   Entry phase.
G   Formal attempts at a strategy stalled or discontinued for the time being.

CS: Conservation Strategy; **DAP:** Draft Action Plan; **EAP:** Environmental Action Plan; **FCCS:** Federal Capital Conservation Strategy; **NAg21:** National Agenda 21; **NCS:** National Conservation Strategy; **NEAP:** National Environmental Action Plan; **NEMAP:** National Environment Management Action Plan; **NES:** National Environmental Strategy. **NSSD:** National Strategy for Sustainable Development; **SCS:** State Conservation Strategy.

Chart B: Development of Selected Strategies for Sustainability in Africa

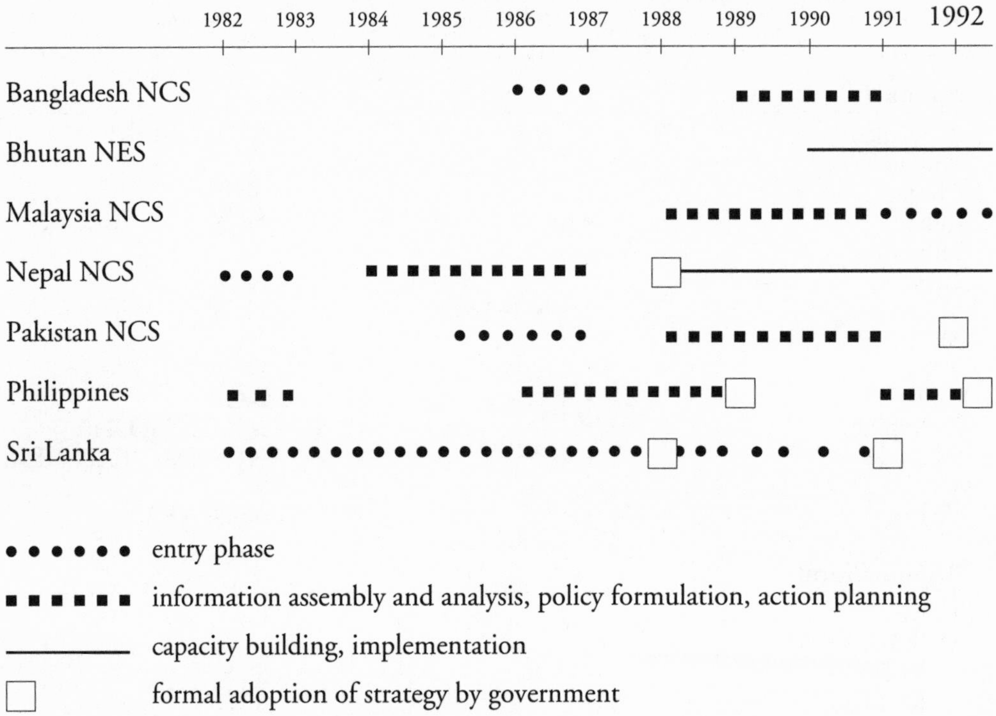

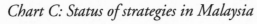

| | 1982 | 1983 | 1984 | 1985 | 1986 | 1987 | 1988 | 1989 | 1990 | 1991 | 1992 |

Bangladesh NCS   ● ● ● ●   ■ ■ ■ ■ ■ ■

Bhutan NES   ——————————

Malaysia NCS   ■ ■ ■ ■ ■ ■ ■ ■ ■ ■ ■ ● ● ● ●

Nepal NCS   ● ● ● ●   ■ ■ ■ ■ ■ ■ ■ ■ ■   □——————————

Pakistan NCS   ● ● ● ● ● ●   ■ ■ ■ ■ ■ ■ ■   □

Philippines   ■ ■ ■   ■ ■ ■ ■ ■ ■ ■ ■ □   ■ ■ ■ □

Sri Lanka   ● ● ● ● ● ● ● ● ● ● ● ● ● ● ● ● □ ● ● ● ● ● ● □

● ● ● ● ● ●   entry phase

■ ■ ■ ■ ■ ■   information assembly and analysis, policy formulation, action planning

——————   capacity building, implementation

□   formal adoption of strategy by government

Chart C: Status of strategies in Malaysia

Strategy	Type	Year
Negeri Sembilan	state	1982
Melaka	state	1983
Terengganu	state	1983
Kedah	state	1984
Perlis	state	1984
Sarawak	state	1985
Selangor	state	1988
Kuala Lumpur	local	1990
Kelantan	state	1991
Sabah	state	1992

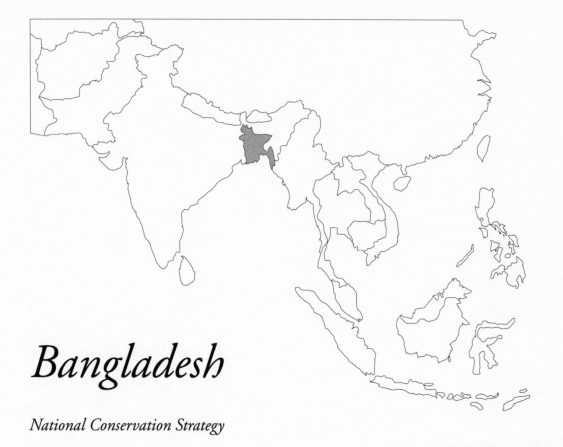

Bangladesh

National Conservation Strategy

Haroun Er Rashid

Population: 110.6 million; **Land area:** 144 000 square kilometres; **Ecological zones:** vast, low-lying alluvial plain; **Climate:** tropical monsoon, main rainy season June to September; **Annual rainfall:** 1000–3810 mm; **Forest area:** 9000 square kilometres; **GNP per capita:** US$ 220; **Main industry:** agriculture, jute, paper, aluminum, textiles; **ODA received per capita:** US$ 14.8; **Population growth rate:** 1.9 per cent; **Life expectancy:** 51 years; **Adult illiteracy:** 65 per cent; **Access to safe water:** 78 per cent; **Access to health care:** 74 per cent; **Access to sanitation:** 12 per cent

1 Introduction

Over the past five years in Bangladesh, pressure from multi-lateral banks and bilateral aid agencies to undertake a range of environment and resource plans has resulted in a series of environmental strategy documents and other reports. They include a National Conservation Strategy, two National Environmental Management Plans, and several natural resource status reports. Neither the NCS nor the NEMAPs have been formally adopted by government. This case study focuses largely on the NCS.

Bangladesh's experience illustrates how strategies can become marginalized if they are not linked to key planning and economic development ministries, and if they do not initially establish credibility and momentum from a broad base of interests. Although a comprehensive process of background papers was undertaken, and attempts were made to set up a task force for its supervision, these mechanisms could not be sustained.

Some NCS participants believe that the Bangladesh NCS may have been premature. They suggest that what was needed initially was a strong programme of environmental awareness to build the conceptual base and support for strategy development. Only then could serious strategy preparation take place.

2 Scope and Objectives

The NCS was expected to identify the obstacles to conservation and sustainable development; and prescribe action to overcome them in an integrated, cost-effective manner. The terms of reference called for the establishment of links between conservation and the national development goals of Bangladesh.

Undertaken in two phases, the strategy aimed to incorporate environmental considerations into the development planning process. It proposed to do this by developing a framework to address natural resource conflicts occurring in the course of socio-economic development. The duties and responsibilities of all relevant ministries were to be clearly spelled out in this framework.

The strategy covers the following sectors:

- agriculture;
- conservation of genetic resources;
- cultural heritage;
- energy and minerals;
- environmental education and awareness;
- environmental pollution;
- fishery;
- forestry and forest conservation;
- health and sanitation;
- human settlement and urban development;

- industry;
- international dimensions;
- land management;
- livestock;
- natural hazards;
- population;
- rural development and NGO activities;
- transportation;
- water resources and flood control; and
- wildlife management and protected areas.

The major objective of the NCS is to provide a guide for development practitioners on the means to preserve or improve the environment while pursuing the goal of sustainable development. The objectives of NCS Phase II as stated in the Technical Assistance Project Proforma (TAPP) are:

- to collect and analyze data on key socio-economic indicators that have relevance in influencing environment and development; and
- to formulate policy and guidelines and prepare a document for proper utilization of natural resources on a sustainable basis without impairing the ecological basis.

3 Relationship to Development Planning

Although the project document authorizing expenditures for strategy

preparation was approved by the planning commission, there were no formal links between the NCS and the existing planning and decision-making system in Bangladesh. The NCS was intended to provide a direct input to the national economic planning process, but this has not happened. Future work on the NCS is intended to contribute to the fourth five-year plan.

4 Strategy Development

Two initiatives contributed to the decision to undertake the Bangladesh NCS: the 1980 World Conservation Strategy and a 1984 request from NORAD to IUCN to undertake a state of environment report for Bangladesh. In the appraisal mission for this report, recommendations for a National Conservation Strategy were made to the Department of Environmental Pollution Control (DEPC). Unfortunately the DEPC had a limited mandate within government, which initially did not endorse the recommendation.

However, with the assistance of IUCN, interest in the NCS was revived within government and the development assistance community. This was done mainly by emphasizing the magnitude of conservation and development problems in Bangladesh and the need for strategic planning to address them. Environment and development issues were also receiving a great deal of attention from donors and the government at that time.

In 1986 another mission was undertaken, during which high-level consultation was carried out within the government. In September of that year, a seminar on Conservation for Development was held in Dhaka, cosponsored by IUCN and the Bangladesh Centre for Advanced Studies.

The seminar brought together representatives of government, including the Ministers for Agriculture and Forestry, Irrigation, Water Resources and Flood Control, officials from the planning commission, NGOs, and donor representatives. The seminar examined development activities in key sectors of the economy and reiterated the need for an overall environment policy for Bangladesh.

Recommendations from the seminar included:

- an NCS for Bangladesh should be developed with the support of government at a high level;
- the decision to proceed with an NCS should be endorsed by the head of state;
- a high-level NCS task force should be appointed, consisting of representatives from government and the private sector, NGOs and the scientific community;

- an NCS secretariat should be established by government to assist the task force, with IUCN providing technical expertise; and
- the task force should prepare a proposal for government approval within six months.

The government signed a memorandum of understanding with IUCN in 1987, requesting its help to prepare the NCS. NORAD agreed to support the development of the NCS process. It was agreed that the NCS secretariat would be established with the Bangladesh Agricultural Research Council (BARC) as the focal point for strategy preparation.

The NCS was prepared in two phases. Phase I (eight months during 1987) was coordinated by BARC. An expatriate advisor, a national consultant and a secretary made up the secretariat staff. This phase produced a prospectus, with an overview of environmental issues and the status of natural resource use and degradation; and spelled out the organization and methodology for Phase II, including a work plan. The prospectus identified 20 areas, including major economic development sectors, and likely environmental issues in each area.

A workshop planned to review the prospectus could not be held due to political unrest in the country.

Consequently, the prospectus did not benefit from peer review. Also, because it was not circulated for discussion, the issues it raised and the rationale for a Bangladesh NCS were not exposed to a wide audience. Thus an opportunity was missed for attracting the support of the scientific community, civil servants and NGOs.

The Ministry of Agriculture and Forests had overall responsibility for the NCS until the creation of the Ministry of Environment and Forests in 1989. Between January 1988, when Phase I ended, and September 1989, when Phase II began, the Ministry of Agriculture and Forests set up a task force of 22 secretary-level members of concerned ministries. Chaired by the Minister for Agriculture and Forests, the task force was to oversee strategy preparation, review products and provide overall guidance. The secretary of the task force was the Director (Forestry) of BARC, which housed the NCS Secretariat.

The task force never met, however, and the entire burden of administration and guidance of the project fell to BARC. By default, the Secretary of the Ministry of Environment and Forests acted as key decision-maker for the NCS. In later stages, he chaired meetings of an ad hoc steering committee that reviewed the progress of strategy preparation. The committee consisted of the Chief

Conservator of Forests, the Director of the Department of Environment, the Secretary of the Task Force and the expatriate resident advisor.

The expatriate advisor had the overall responsibility for the day-to-day running of the NCS secretariat, reporting to the Executive Vice-chair of BARC. Establishing the secretariat began in October 1989; but, due to personality problems and inertia, it took more than a year to reach its complement, which comprised the expatriate resident advisor, a national consultant, two junior technical officers, an office assistant, secretary and a driver.

The secretary of the task force provided liaison between the NCS Secretariat and BARC, and with government and semi-governmental institutions.

To provide background information for analysis in the strategy document, 20 background papers were undertaken by selected national consultants. The first draft of each background paper was reviewed by the expatriate advisor; the second draft was reviewed by a qualified person in the relevant discipline. It was then finalized by the consultant.

A lack of national staff for three positions in the first year of the project made it difficult to keep to the work plan. Consultants were given three months to review the sector status, identify issues in policy, legislation and management areas, and propose ways to resolve current or potential issues. None of the consultants met the deadline; even after 12 months, some consultancies were not completed. Some of the papers were of poor quality when finally completed. In retrospect, the contracts with authors could have been much more clear with respect to time and product.

As part of the consensus-building process, seven sectoral workshops were held to present sectoral write-ups prepared by the NCS secretariat. These sectors were:

- land resources;
- genetic diversity;
- forestry;
- wildlife;
- agriculture;
- energy and minerals; and
- fisheries and water resources.

Experts, senior government officials representing key institutions and academics in related fields attended these workshops. In most cases consensus was the basis of agreement. In a few technical areas the decision of the lead agency was accepted. The sectoral write-ups were discussed in detail in these workshops, revised, and included in the draft NCS document. Due to time constraints, write-ups prepared by the secretariat on other

sectors could not be presented in sectoral workshops.

The first draft of the NCS document was presented in a two-day national workshop held in August, 1991. In the inaugural session, Mr Abdullah Al-Noman, State Minister for the Ministry of Environment and Forests and the Ministry of Fisheries and Livestock as the Chief Guest, confirmed the government's commitment to the NCS. Experts, senior government officials and academics commented on the draft in organized discussions.

At the same time, the draft NCS document was circulated to all ministries through the sponsoring Ministry of Environment and Forests (MOEF) for their comments. Comments were received from ten of them.

A second draft of the NCS document was prepared in 1991 and circulated through MOEF; further comments were received from twelve ministries.

In 1993 cabinet ministers took the unprecedented step of holding their own seminar on the second draft of the NCS document. However, they were unable to approve it due to objections from the Ministry of Industries.

There was little substantive participation in NCS preparation by government agencies, NGOs or semi-governmental institutions, and almost no participation from the private sector. Opportunities for consultation were limited to the workshops. Although the NCS task force had a broad spectrum of appointed representatives, it never met.

Although the views of NGOs were solicited by mail, few responded. The Environmental Journalists Forum was requested to provide publicity and public awareness articles, but did not do so.

There were no pilot projects and very little in the way of field visits to sound out public opinion. The NCS document is largely the product of a group of academics and government officials.

There were no requirements to monitor and evaluate the NCS. It was assumed that the IUCN Country Office and MOEF would do this, but due to lack of project funding they did not.

National Environmental Management Action Plan

A NEMAP was requested by MOEF to outline projects and programmes that could alleviate environmental degradation. It was intended to complement the NCS document. The NCS was conceived as providing an overview of issues and general policy guidance; the NEMAP as providing an action plan for specific projects.

Work on the NEMAP began well before the NCS document was complete, with funding from UNDP. It was prepared by a small team of Bangladeshi experts. However, the project ran out of funds and the NEMAP was never completed. Later, a second NEMAP was started, again with UNDP funding. It remains a confidential draft and has not been adopted.

5 *Implementation and results*

The NCS secretariat envisaged that different ministries would implement the NCS, according to guidelines in the sixth chapter of the document. This chapter covers all 18 sectors and relevant government agencies. However, because cabinet has not approved the strategy and the government agencies concerned were insufficiently involved in its development, this has not happened.

The NCS has been overshadowed and ignored by the Bangladesh Flood Action Plan. In addition, the fact that the NCS was marginalized within government and not internalized in key government agencies has resulted in duplication by parallel exercises. The Association of Development Agencies in Bangladesh (ADAB), through its Environment Advisory Group, produced the document *Environmental Problems in Bangladesh: An NGO Perspective for Policies and Action.* (ADAB Environmental Advisory Group,

August 1990, Dhaka, Bangladesh). The United States Agency for International Development (USAID) produced *Bangladesh: Environment and Natural Resources Assessment* in 1990. The MOEF also prepared a separate environmental policy.

IUCN did not have the resources to continue supporting the NCS process, did not publicize it, and left participants feeling somewhat abandoned. In 1992, NORAD, which until then had backed IUCN's involvement, chose to provide funds for NCS implementation directly to the government. Many donor agencies were aware of the NCS preparation and were supportive of the outcome, yet others (such as USAID) proceeded to mount environmental studies of their own.

6 Lessons learned

Despite the upsurge of interest in environment and development issues in Bangladesh by various donor agencies, such as CIDA, the Danish International Development Agency (DANIDA), NORAD, SIDA and USAID, some participants in the NCS feel it may have been premature to undertake a strategy. The problems with Phases I and II of the NCS process, the human and financial constraints, and the absence of a sound database on resources, militated against a successful NCS process.

In addition, the experience and influence of other donor-supported initiatives like the Flood Action Plan indicated that the government might not be able to take control of independent strategic planning. The government seemed to be unduly influenced by opportunities for new initiatives, quickly abandoning one exercise in favour of the next.

Perhaps a major process of consciousness-raising and environmental education should first have been undertaken to plant the seeds of the NCS concept. Strategy preparation could have followed once interest and commitment had been generated.

The problem may have been due not so much to a premature NCS process, but to mistakes that could have been avoided or corrected, including the following:

- Dialogue on the issues among policy-makers, decision-makers, resource users and the public was very weak in the Bangladesh NCS. A wide participation programme could have developed a higher profile and level of awareness of the NCS, and given it the momentum and support needed for its adoption and implementation. As it stands, the NCS has been marginalized by other initiatives and has fallen into obscurity.
- The failure of the task force to function left a void in the stewardship of strategy preparation. Without the backing of

key government officials, many government institutions were either slow or not interested in participating in NCS preparation.

- Continuity and suitability of staffing was a problem through Phase I and half of Phase II. Some seconded staff were not available when required by the secretariat, while others were unfamiliar with NCS concepts and thus ineffective.

- The failure of the schedule for background papers caused considerable delay and loss of momentum in strategy preparation. In retrospect, instead of commissioning papers from consultants, it might have been more productive to have worked through small groups assigned to each sector, with greater participation from government institutions responsible for the sector.

- The choice of BARC as a focal point for the NCS was a mistake, since it was outside the main planning and development system and had little influence on it.

- Lack of continuity between phases of the NCS resulted in a loss of

momentum. Changes in staff resulted in an uneven understanding of the concepts and objectives of an NCS among seconded staff. A comprehensive briefing course could have helped all national staff involved in NCS preparation. In addition, secondments from key government institutions responsible for planning or development could have ensured that the NCS messages and concepts were carried back to these institutions when staff returned.

The multitude of overlapping environmental exercises indicate that there is little coordination of donor-sponsored efforts or government initiatives. Bangladesh is overrun with donor assistance and constantly-changing project focus. The government, multilateral and bilateral agencies — as well as international NGOs such as IUCN — do not behave as if they have a strategic sense of what they are doing. They start initiatives that duplicate existing work, and abandon initiatives when they most need support. The NCS was a victim of this lack of strategy.

7	*Chronology*

1980   World Conservation Strategy.

1984   NORAD asks IUCN to prepare a State of Environment Report for Bangladesh. This report recommends the development of a National Conservation Strategy.

1985   IUCN visit to discuss the NCS.

1986   A proposal for an NCS is developed by the Department of Environmental Pollution Control (DEPC) but is not approved. IUCN resident representative meets with senior officials on the NCS proposal and receives positive interest from government. A "Conservation for Development" workshop, cosponsored by IUCN and BARC, is held in Dhaka with good participation and interest from senior officials and government representatives. It recommends that an NCS for Bangladesh be undertaken over six months with IUCN assistance. A follow-up meeting is held, chaired by the Secretary, Ministry of Agriculture and Forests, and a working group is established to draw up proposals for strategy preparation.

1987   Memorandum of Undertanding (MOU) signed with IUCN to assist in preparing an NCS. Phase I: May to December 1987, preparation of a prospectus for an NCS. NCS Secretariat established at BARC. Prospectus completed but not widely reviewed. Workshop for review cancelled due to political unrest in country.

1988   Ministry of Agriculture sets up a 22-person task force to oversee NCS development with the Minister for Agriculture and Forests as chair. The task force never meets.

1989   Phase II NCS: October 1989 to September 1991.

1990   A NEMAP is undertaken with UNDP support. USAID prepares an Environmental and Natural Resources Assessment while NCS is being prepared. ADAB undertakes a report *(Environmental Problems in Bangladesh: An NGO Perspective for Policies and Action.* ADAB Environment Advisory Group, August 1990, Dhaka, Bangladesh). The Ministry of Environment and Forests prepares its own environmental policy.

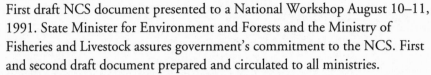

1991   First draft NCS document presented to a National Workshop August 10–11, 1991. State Minister for Environment and Forests and the Ministry of Fisheries and Livestock assures government's commitment to the NCS. First and second draft document prepared and circulated to all ministries.

1992   IUCN ceases to support NCS. NORAD makes policy decision to channel funds only through government for further NCS work. Cabinet holds seminar on second draft NCS document but does not approve it due to objections from the Ministry of Industries.

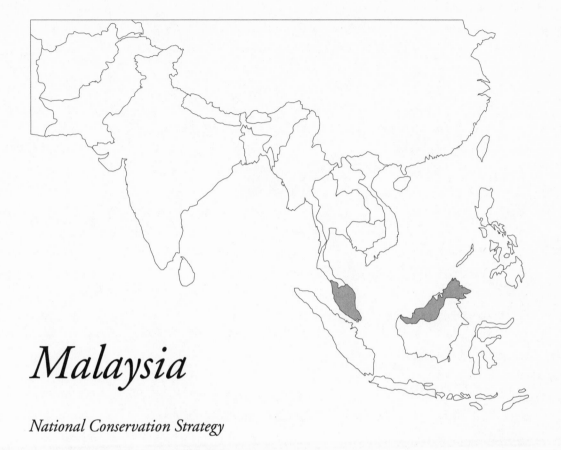

Malaysia

National Conservation Strategy

ISHAK BIN ARIFFIN AND GEOFFREY DAVIDSON

Population: 18.2 million; **Land area:** 330 000 square kilometres; **Ecological zones:** mostly tropical rainforest and mangrove swamp, mountain chain and coastal plains, swampy coastal belt; **Climate:** tropical, strongly influenced by monsoon winds; **Annual rainfall:** 260–800 mm; **Forest area:** 210 000 square kilometres; **GNP per capita:** US$ 2520; **Main industry:** tin, rubber, timber, fishing; **ODA received per capita:** US$ 15.9; **Population growth rate:** 2.2 per cent; **Life expectancy:** 71 years; **Adult illiteracy:** 22 per cent; **Access to safe water:** 78 per cent; **Access to health care:** 88 per cent; **Access to sanitation:** 94 per cent

1 Introduction

Malaysia was one of the first countries to formulate conservation strategies following the publication of the World Conservation Strategy in 1980. State strategies have been prepared in nine of Malaysia's thirteen states, as well as a strategy for the Kuala Lumpur Federal Territory; and a National Conservation Strategy (NCS) has been developed. The nine state strategies are:

Early strategies (1982–1984)

- Negeri Sembilan, 1982;
- Melaka, 1983;
- Terengganu, 1983;
- Kedah, 1984; and
- Perlis, 1984.

Later strategies (1985–1992)

- Sarawak, 1985;
- Selangor, 1988;
- Kelantan, 1991; and
- Sabah, 1992.

Work on the Kuala Lumpur strategy began in 1989, and on the NCS in 1993.

The initiative for the state strategies came from the World Wide Fund for Nature, Malaysia (WWF-M), which met the costs of the first five efforts. From the Sarawak strategy on, however, WWF-M has been retained by state and national governments only as a consultant for the development of strategies. The governments concerned have paid for the later strategies. Funding for all but one of the strategies (Sabah) has come entirely from within Malaysia, with no international assistance.

The role of WWF-M is a unusual example of an NGO preparing essentially governmental strategies that otherwise had little non-governmental influence. The early strategies were initiated by WWF-M and prepared with negligible involvement by the governments. As a result, governments were unfamiliar with the conservation strategy concept, were not persuaded of the need, and lacked an incentive to implement it. By contrast, the NCS, and the Selangor, Kelantan, Sabah, and Kuala Lumpur strategies were prepared under contract to, and with the direct involvement of, the governments. As a result, the governments are more committed to these strategies and have started to implement all five.

2 Scope and Objectives

State Strategies

Although the central theme of all the strategies has been the relationship between conservation and development,

the early state strategies differ in scope from the later ones. The early strategies were primarily concerned with providing a framework for ecological sustainability and for maintaining and enhancing the aesthetic qualities of wildlife and scenery. They tended to make general recommendations about some of the more important issues such as agriculture, forestry, water, wildlife, pollution and human settlements. They focused mainly on the negative impacts of development. The language of the strategy documents tends to be rather scientific and sometimes condescending, with little attention to the socio-economic aspects of conservation or natural resource management.

The scope of the later state strategies is more broad. They include issues not addressed in the early strategies, such as the administrative and legal aspects of resource use. As well as providing a strategic planning framework, they also address specific problems and discuss alternative management and policy responses, which are consolidated in an action plan.

In particular, the later strategies place more emphasis on cross-sector aspects and the need to sensitize government officials to the complexities of conservation issues.

National Conservation Strategy

The objective of the NCS is providing a strategic framework to guide the implementation of the principles of sustainable development (as contained in: World Commission on Environment and Development, 1987. *Our Common Future*. Oxford University Press, Oxford). The NCS covers all aspects of the use, management and protection of natural resources and the environment. It emphasizes the optimal use of natural resources according to development needs, together with conservation of nature, natural resources and the environment throughout the country. It is intended to provide the overall perspective essential for integrated planning.

The NCS focuses on three groups of issues:

- the administration of natural resources and the environment, including policy formulation, enforcement, and education;
- geographical aspects of resource protection and management, such as the distribution of managed and protected areas; and
- systems for measuring natural resources and the environment, including natural resource accounting and environmental auditing.

The NCS is also intended to provide a process for sensitizing government officials to the role of conservation in sustainable development.

3 Relationship to Development Planning

The relationship of the state strategies to the existing planning system is evolving. Early strategies were peripheral to development planning, but later strategies have been developed in cooperation with the state economic planning units. The extent of this cooperation has varied from state to state. The process of preparing the NCS involved extensive discussion with government planning agencies; and implementation is likely to be coordinated by the economic planning unit in the Prime Minister's Department.

The Sixth Malaysia Plan (1991–1995) includes sections on Conservation and Sustainable Resource Development, and Economic Development and the Environment, and commits the federal government to the development of conservation strategies.

The conservation strategies of Kelantan and Selangor influenced the states' development plans. The governments of Kelantan, Selangor, and Kuala Lumpur have also invited the conservation strategy teams to provide conservation advice on several development projects.

The Sabah Conservation Strategy was initiated by the state government as a result of discussions with the World Bank, and was supported by two UNDP projects.

4 Strategy Development

State Strategies

After the launch of the World Conservation Strategy in 1980, WWF-M approached the federal Ministry of Science, Technology and Environment (MSTE) with a proposal to undertake studies that would lead to a series of conservation strategies for the states of Malaysia.

WWF-M's interest in conservation strategies was prompted by a range of environmental problems resulting from the accelerating rate of development in Malaysia. These included forest clearance for agricultural development schemes; the impact of extensive logging on soil, water and species; increasing urban and industrial pollution; and damage to fisheries due to clearance of mangroves.

Initially it was proposed that all thirteen states would be covered in five years. To

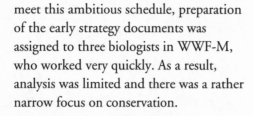

meet this ambitious schedule, preparation of the early strategy documents was assigned to three biologists in WWF-M, who worked very quickly. As a result, analysis was limited and there was a rather narrow focus on conservation.

The strategy team, based in Kuala Lumpur, visited each state only for short periods, and had few working contacts with the officials concerned with development issues. In addition, WWF-M paid all the costs of strategy preparation, providing the states with a conservation strategy document. The state governments made no financial or policy commitment to the strategies, and had no substantive involvement in their preparation.

After completing the first five strategy documents, WWF-M concluded that more detailed work was necessary. This meant that it could no longer meet all of the costs. Since then (1985), state strategies have been produced with financial support from the state governments. WWF-M provided a technical consultancy service and, in some cases, a small financial contribution.

The teams preparing the later strategies have been based in the states and have operated from, or in close liaison with, government offices. They have worked jointly with the local state or federal government officials and at least one member of the team has been drawn from

the economic planning unit. Over the years, government involvement has grown from assigning a liaison officer to providing significant technical support.

The response of the state governments to the idea of conservation strategies has varied, depending upon the environmental problems, the attitudes of officials, and the way the idea was introduced. In the early years, many state governments, although aware of environmental issues, found no pressing reason to undertake a conservation strategy. They had little interest in conservation, partly because the federal government controlled many aspects of natural resources. Their acceptance of WWF-M's offer was, to a considerable extent, a token gesture. Consequently, most of the pre-1985 strategy documents had little impact and their ideas were never taken up by the state governments. Only in Perlis was the strategy document followed up to any extent, when the state government asked WWF-M to participate in the review of the state master plan.

In the mid-1980s, the situation began to change. The Sarawak strategy document was produced as a result of direct collaboration between WWF-M and the state planning unit. WWF-M was also asked to assist in redrafting the state's Natural Resource Ordinance, which had been identified as a key vehicle for implementation of the conservation strategy. (Later, WWF-M's involvement in the Sarawak strategy was halted in response to WWF International's involvement in the tropical forestry debate. This situation has since improved.)

This more positive relationship with a state government, and the neglect of the early strategy documents, led WWF-M to raise the issue of state government participation with the Prime Minister's Science Advisor and the Director General of the Economic Planning Unit (EPU) in the Prime Minister's Department. Both of these individuals had endorsed the conservation strategy idea.

As a result, in 1986 the National Seminar on Conservation for Developmen(NSCD) t was sponsored by the EPU, the Prime Minister's Science Office, the Department of the Environment, and *Institut Tadbiran Awam Negara Malaysia* (ITAN). This seminar explained to state and federal officials the importance of conservation for development and the relevance of WWF-M's Conservation Strategy Malaysia project to the Fifth Malaysia Plan. Participants concluded that WWF-M should continue to draw up state strategies, but in closer collaboration with the state economic planning units or their equivalents, and that the state governments should provide the funds.

The first signs that the seminar had been effective came the same year when the Selangor government agreed to fully fund the state's conservation strategy study. All strategies since then have been wholly funded by the government concerned. Preparation of each of the later strategies has involved detailed discussion with the state economic planning unit and a workshop with state government officials to reach agreement on the draft document. WWF-M has remained largely responsible for the actual drafting, although in Selangor and Kelantan, government staff were involved in formulating the strategy.

Participation in strategy development has been largely limited to governments, although some universities, NGOs, and private companies have been invited to join discussions. Draft strategy documents are classified as confidential by the governments.

National Conservation Strategy

Awareness of the need for an NCS grew during the 1980s, partly as a result of experience with the state strategies. The Fifth Malaysia Plan (1985–1990) highlighted the growing importance of protection of the environment against degradation, especially over-exploitation of natural resources and pollution. The plan stressed the need to incorporate preventive environmental action into the development process. Preparation for the UN Conference on Environment and

Development also increased awareness.

As a result of discussions between the EPU in the Prime Minister's Department and WWF-M, a technical working group was convened. It agreed that an NCS should be prepared and implementation begin during the Sixth Malaysia Plan.

The NCS document was prepared by WWF-M as a consultancy project for the Regional Economic Section of the EPU. The preparatory process was guided by two bodies: a steering committee of representatives of federal ministries and state economic planning units; and a technical committee of representatives of government departments and universities. The secretariat for the steering committee was the Regional Economics Section of EPU; for the technical committee it was the Environmental Conservation and Management Section of the Ministry of Science, Technology and Environment.

Preparation of the NCS was more consultative than it had been for the state strategies. Background papers were prepared by authors from 13 organizations within universities, government departments and the private sector. Special studies on natural resource accounting were undertaken by consultants from Harvard's Institute of International Development, the

Agricultural University of Malaysia, and the private sector.

The state economic planning units organized a series of workshops around the country to familiarize government staff with the NCS preparation process. These brought together staff from government agencies and some private bodies; they were briefed on the NCS, its background, process and output, and then involved in questions and discussions. The workshops were followed by meetings with individuals from each state. In this way, more than 200 people from almost 150 departments were consulted on the preparation of the NCS document.

5 Implementation and Results

State Strategies

Except for Perlis's, the early strategies did not progress beyond the document stage; and the documents themselves appear to have had little impact. Although 30 copies of each strategy were presented to the relevant state government when completed, a follow-up project in 1989 found that most had disappeared without trace and that there was no recollection of their development or of the ideas they had introduced.

In Perlis, the strategy document was used in reviewing development plans. More recently, the state government and WWF-M have started working together on conservation of limestone hill plants.

WWF-M is trying to promote implementation in the other 'early' states. In Kedah, for example, it is working with the Forestry Department on mangrove conservation.

By contrast, four of the five later strategies (all except Sarawak) are beginning to be implemented, albeit modestly. In Selangor, the government has appointed an environmental officer and developed a number of projects and action plans concerned with mangrove and aquaculture development, peat swamp forests and freshwater fish conservation. In Kelantan, a state limestone policy is being developed (limestone hills are rich in endemic plants). In Kuala Lumpur, the strategy has been accepted as a guide for future development: the main areas of implementation to date have been urban landscaping and bringing wildlife back into the city.

National Conservation Strategy

Implementation of the NCS began before its official approval. As commissioning agency, the EPU is implementing work on natural resource accounting and environmental auditing. It is also considering financial mechanisms between the federal and state governments that could be used as tools for sustainable development.

All government agencies responsible for aspects of natural resources and the environment are expected to implement the strategy, leaving the EPU responsible for coordination. The EPU is well equipped for this role since it has a strong planning capability, exists outside the rigid structure of sectoral ministries and departments, and already leads an inter-agency planning group. At present, a great deal of coordination is sought informally. Although this approach has achieved compromise among conflicting interests, it has sometimes been at the expense of necessary policy changes.

The federal government is committed to establishing a national council for the environment, which will be responsible for monitoring and evaluating NCS implementation.

6 Lessons Learned

Governments are the main users of strategies in Malaysia. It is essential that they participate actively in the development of the strategies, so that they will be committed to them, understand them, develop the capacity to implement them, and actually carry them out.

Experience with strategies elsewhere shows that active participation includes:

- commissioning the strategy and, as far as possible, paying for it;
- committing agencies and staff to its preparation and implementation; and
- integrating the strategy with the rest of government policy-making and planning.

The need for such participation is made clear by the fate of the early state strategies. State governments did not commission or pay for the strategy documents or participate in their preparation. As a result, four of the five strategy documents were effectively ignored and the fifth (Perlis) led to only minimal action.

All the later strategies were commissioned and funded by the governments con-cerned. All the governments contributed at least one staff member of the economic planning unit, or its equivalent, to the team preparing the strategy document. Consequently, the prospects of implemen-tation are brighter; and all the strategies are being implemented, although not yet to any great extent.

Except in the case of the NCS and the Kelantan strategy, however, only a few

government agencies and staff were deeply involved in preparing the strategy documents. It is doubtful that even the later state strategies are well-integrated with the policy-making machinery of the governments concerned. Possibly, WWF-M allowed the governments to rely on it too much, instead of ensuring deeper governmental involvement even at the cost of slower progress. Consequently, considerable effort is still needed to promote each strategy within government and ensure its implementation. WWF-M has recognized this and started a conservation strategy implementation programme.

In addition to government input, full participation by a wide range of non-government representatives is generally regarded as essential for an effective strategy. Apart from WWF-M's role as a consultant, non-governmental participation has been low in the NCS and very low in the state strategies. This is consistent with the style of many govern-ments; the effect it will have on progress remains to be seen. Strategies are evolutionary processes; participation can be widened as the strategies develop. At this stage, deepening participation within government is probably more important.

Many government officials still perceive conservation to be solely concerned with wildlife issues and in conflict with economic development. Greater involvement in conservation strategies could help to overcome this perception. WWF-M has also had to contend with the perception that it has conflicting national and international roles, especially with respect to campaigns by international NGOs against tropical forest logging. This has been a particular problem since state and federal governments are very sensitive to charges of over-exploitation of the natural resource base.

This sensitivity, and the nature of WWF-M's role as a consultant to government, have constrained WWF-M to a relatively low-key approach. In Malaysia, it is doubtful that conservation strategies could have been encouraged through a more public process. After ten years of working with governments, WWF-M is now seen as a source of constructive, independent advice, and not as a threat. The role that WWF-M has accepted is an interesting adjustment of the strategy development process to the conditions of a society.

7	*Chronology*

1976	Third Malaysia Plan recognizes need for a national environmental policy, environmental education, EIA, greater attention to control of pollution and management, and conservation of natural resources and ecosystems.
1980	WCS leads to discussions between WWF-M and the federal MSTE of WWF-M's proposal for studies to develop a series of conservation strategies for the states of Malaysia with the studies being financed by WWF-M.
1982	State strategy document completed for Negeri Sembilan. No follow up by state government.
1983	State strategy documents completed for Melaka and Terengganu. Neither followed up by state governments.
1984	State strategy documents completed for Perlis and Kedah. Some follow up by Perlis; none by Kedah.
1985	Sarawak strategy document completed after first collaboration between WWF-M strategy formulation team and a state planning unit.
1986	Initial implementation of Perlis strategy through WWF-M assistance in review of the state Master Plan; and of Sarawak strategy, with WWF-M support for redrafting state Natural Resource Ordinance. WWF-M's involvement halted due to links with international NGOs involved in tropical forestry controversy. NSCD, attended by state and federal government, confirms need for strategies and WWF-M's role in strategy preparation as consultant, with most costs met by state governments. Agreement that strategy formulation should have closer collaboration with government departments.
1988	Selangor and Kuala Lumpur Federal Territory Strategy documents completed. Some implementation begun of both strategies.
1991	Kelantan strategy document completed with close involvement of state government staff. Sixth Malaysia Plan includes a specific commitment to the development of conservation strategies.
1992	Sabah Strategy document completed, implementation begins. UNCED leads to wider public support for conservation by the public and politicians.
1993	National Conservation Strategy document completed and implementation begun. Kelantan strategy implementation begun.

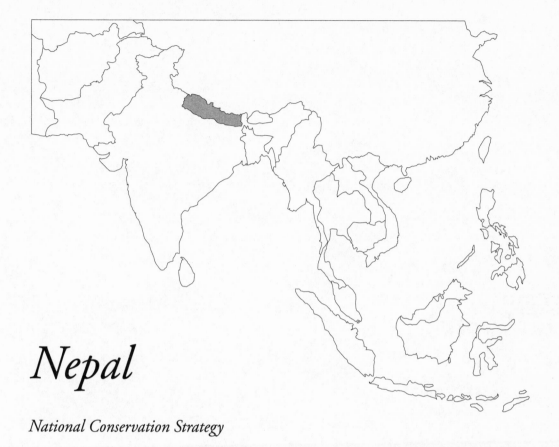

Nepal

National Conservation Strategy

RAM B KHADKA AND JOHN MCEACHERN

Population: 19.4 million; **Land area:** 141 000 square kilometres; **Ecological zones:** landlocked country with high fertile valleys, glaciated peaks of the Himalayas; **Climate:** varies from subtropical lowland to alpine; **Annual rainfall:** 890–1778 mm; **Forest area:** 21 000 square kilometres; **GNP per capita:** US$ 180; **Main industry:** agriculture, coal, hydro-electric power, tourism; **ODA received per capita:** US$ 23.4; **Population growth rate:** 2.5 per cent; **Life expectancy:** 53 years; **Adult illiteracy:** 74 per cent; **Access to safe water:** 37 per cent; **Access to sanitation:** 6 per cent

1 Introduction

In 1982 Nepal embarked on an NCS process, with the preparation of a prospectus. An NCS document was completed in 1987 and implementation, coordinated by the National Planning Commission (NPC), began in 1989. Nepal's experience with the NCS process is one of the longest-running in the world and has many lessons that are generally applicable. The NCS has been a major force in nurturing innovation and reform for environmental protection in Nepal, despite difficult institutional barriers.

Preparation of the NCS document included consultation at national and village level throughout the country. Much of the momentum and awareness gained during this period was lost because of delays in endorsing the policy and commencing implementation. Political unrest leading to a revolution in 1990, and regular staff changes within government administration made it difficult to maintain consistency in approach and commitment.

These problems illustrate the importance of continuity and flexibility within the strategy secretariat, and of the need for the document to be prepared concurrently with implementation so that one process reinforces the other. If the action plan component is over-designed it can take initiative from those desk officers responsible for implementation. An action plan that is too detailed soon loses relevance in a volatile political and institutional climate. This emphasizes the need for regular review and adjustment.

The NCS implementation programme has concentrated on building the basic components and skills for an environment management administration in Nepal. It includes developing national systems of environmental impact assessment (EIA) and planning. The positive response to these initiatives justifies the focus on activities that are of widespread and immediate use and have strong support in government and society.

Reform to institutional structures was given limited attention in the early stages of the strategy process to avoid exacerbating tensions among government agencies. In 1992, following three years of implementation, an Environmental Protection Council (EPC) was established. One major contribution to building institutional capacity was the establishment of an Environmental Core Group of officials from various ministries. This helped ensure that awareness of the NCS was widespread throughout the government. It has built up a group of technicians who are trained, who define the policies and who administer them, as has been the case with the EIA guidelines.

The NCS programme is now at the stage when key policy initiatives require legislative expression and need to be more fully integrated within government. The real test comes over the next three years, during the transition from an externally funded project of the NPC to a self-sustaining strategy process at the heart of the development cycle.

2 Scope and Objectives

The objectives of the NCS are to:

- satisfy the material, spiritual and cultural needs of the present and future generations of Nepal;
- ensure the sustainable use of Nepal's land and renewable resources;
- preserve the biological diversity of Nepal in order to maintain the variety of wild species, both plant and animal, and improve the yields and the quality of crops and livestock: and
- maintain essential ecological systems, such as soil regeneration, nutrient recycling and protection and cleansing of water and air.

The strategy document was intended to provide a long-term perspective on natural resource management to meet the country's development needs. Its goal is strengthened management capacity to address the complex causes of resource degradation. It aims to link sustainable

development with conservation; a goal consistent with a Royal Directive calling for basic needs of the people to be met by the year 2000.

The strategy document sets out the results of 18 sectoral and cross-sectoral analyses, on topics including population and human settlement, energy and industrial development, the role of woman and biological diversity.

A seven-part Conservation Action Agenda covers institutions, conservation awareness, policy, organization and administration, research, inventory and directed studies, resource planning and a vanguard programme of integrated village resource management.

3 Relationship to Development Planning

The NCS process is coordinated by the NPC and managed through a Swiss-funded commission project, with IUCN providing technical backing. The NPC is the principal planning agency of government, chaired by the Prime Minister, with advisory, rather than implementation, responsibilities. The NPC's central role has facilitated links between development planning and the NCS process. However, until adequate staffing is provided within the NPC Environment Division, to take over all functions of the NCS project, formal and systematic integration will be constrained. Important advances include the establishment of the EPC, which brings with it obligations to institutionalize the strategy process.

The potential for inter-sectoral coordination in development and environment planning comes through the NPC Environment Division, acting as secretariat to the EPC. Prior to the council, the NPC worked within existing institutional arrangements to demonstrate the value of the NCS in national development and to gain support for the necessary administrative reforms. The commission also concentrated on building cross-cutting policies and capabilities within government that did not impinge directly on sectoral territories such as heritage conservation and environmental assessment. Two ad hoc advisory committees were established by the NPC: Environmental Planning and Assessment and Environmental Education, and these provided informal coordination of NCS implementation activities.

The NCS team was closely involved in formulating Nepal's Eighth National Development Plan. The Eighth Plan (1992–1997) includes a chapter on the environment, as well as environmental components in sector chapters, and recognizes and applies the various conservation principles of the strategy document, especially with respect to managing natural and cultural resources. Sector plans like the master plan for the forestry sector also recognize the NCS.

4 Strategy Development

The Secretary to the Prime Minister's Office attended the World Conservation Strategy (WCS) launch in 1980. Strong endorsement of the WCS by Prince Gyanendra Bir Bikram Shah led to an initiative to formulate an NCS for Nepal. A task force was established in 1982, led by the NPC, the Department of National Parks and Wildlife Conservation, and the Department of Soil Conservation and Watershed Management (DSCWM). Chaired by the Vice-Chair of the NPC, the task force consisted of high-level officials from the fields of national planning and conservation and environment, as well as IUCN advisors.

Late in 1983 a prospectus was produced which reviewed the environmental problems in the country, identified obstacles and priority areas for action, and outlined a work plan for an NCS. It took almost a year for the prospectus to be endorsed by the government; only then could the NPC and DSCWM draw up an agreement with IUCN.

Strategy formulation started in 1985 and lasted almost three years. The NCS Secretariat was established as part of, but situated outside, the NPC. It was staffed by representatives of each of the government agencies involved in the agreement and supported by an expatriate senior advisor from IUCN.

The NCS office's location, away from the NPC building, offered some important advantages at that time. It provided a neutral ground where representatives of government departments and NGOs could discuss the strategy, and helped the NCS process to avoid red tape. It also meant, however, that maintaining the NCS process was left to IUCN rather than government. As a result, government responsibility and commitment to the NCS was slow to develop.

Strategy formulation involved compiling data from a variety of sources and analysis by experts from government, the private sector and academia. The number of full-time staff of the secretariat increased to eight for this work and local consultants were also employed.

The secretariat conducted extensive fieldwork throughout the country. More than 100 meetings were held in villages and towns to explore people's views of resource conservation problems. The secretariat heard from several hundred people, including tenant farmers, land-owner farmers, village and district committees, private business people, industrialists, educators, government administrators and members of parliament, and representatives of NGOs, including women's, farmers' and youth groups. Background papers were also commissioned on 19 key subjects.

The secretariat drafted a strategy document on the basis of the meetings, background papers, and reviews. It was guided by ten criteria:

- to provide a framework for evaluating and modifying development proposals;
- to ensure the fullest use of existing government and NGO institutions;
- to address the four objectives of the NCS;
- to recognize the financial and manpower constraints of line agencies;
- to recognize the nation's dependence upon natural resources;
- to take into account the needs and circumstances of villagers, the landless and land-owners, recognizing that conservation measures that involve extra costs are made impossible by poverty;
- to use the existing village and district structures in line with the government's decentralization policy;
- to provide a focal point for existing resource management activities and develop these into integrated resource management plans;
- to provide for effective public participation in the preparation of the strategy; and

- to maintain the spiritual and cultural values fundamental to the Nepalese people.

The NCS document went through four drafts. It was first reviewed by the authors of the background papers, then by a 22-member specialist panel, then by a meeting of senior government officials, and finally through three meetings of secretaries to all ministries, the vice-chancellors of Tribhuvan University and the Royal Nepal Academy of Science and Technology. The final version was completed at the end of 1987, endorsed by the government in March 1988 and published in 1989.

5 Implementation and Results

NCS Implementation Project

Implementation did not begin until 1989, two years after document completion, so momentum was lost. The political situation was also uncertain, with four changes of government between 1989 and 1991. The government asked IUCN-Nepal to play a major role in promoting implementation, but for the first two years there was no formal memorandum of understanding. This was not entirely a disadvantage since it freed the secretariat from the immediate demands of government and allowed it to operate informally. That helped avoid rivalries that might have developed from a more formal approach to cooperation.

The secretariat was established to staff the NPC NCS implementation project. The NPC has advisory status within the Prime Minister's department. It is the only truly cross-sector agency in government and is well-situated to facilitate access to all other ministries and departments. The implementation project is staffed by locally recruited experts (some seconded from government and academia) and one IUCN expatriat advisor. There are 25 technical staff, most with expertise in ecology, environmental management and environmental engineering, plus 20 support staff. The project director also heads the Environmental Division within NPC. The NPC Member for Environment, the equivalent of a ministerial appointee, chairs the weekly management committee meetings, which include the project director and the IUCN advisor.

The implementation process is guided by the EPC, which acts as a steering committee. The council, established in 1992, is chaired by the Prime Minister; it has ten ministers among its members. All ministries and agencies with environmental concerns are represented. The Environment Division of the NPC is secretariat to the council.

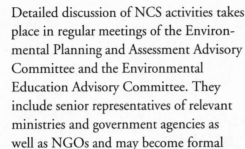

Detailed discussion of NCS activities takes place in regular meetings of the Environmental Planning and Assessment Advisory Committee and the Environmental Education Advisory Committee. They include senior representatives of relevant ministries and government agencies as well as NGOs and may become formal working committees of the EPC.

Implementation

The NCS document recognizes that it is neither appropriate nor feasible for the government to be totally responsible for implementation. Instead, there is strong emphasis on involving individual land users, village and district government institutions, the private sector and NGOs.

The implementation project has not tried to carry out all of the document's recommendations. Some, in fact, were no longer relevant by the time implementation began.

The project has avoided institutional issues that were likely to create conflict among government departments. Inter-ministerial relations are sensitive, and it was felt that to start by addressing them at a time of great political change could lead to rejection of the entire NCS process. Instead, the project focused on gaps in the existing responsibilities of government departments and has worked to simulate

inter-ministerial cooperation in these areas. Clearly-felt needs shared across government and by society as a whole, such as pollution control, environmental impact assessment and environmental education, determined areas in the NCS framework that would receive the attention of the NCS Secretariat. At the same time, individual ministries were encouraged to respond to priority sectoral concerns of the NCS.

The development of an Environmental Core Group (ECG) has been at the heart of the secretariat's approach to implementation. This group has grown to a network of more than 90 senior officials and technical specialists from 20 ministries and departments as well as from all divisions of the NPC. The ECG mandate is to develop, test and apply new environmental policies and procedures. The group has been the focus of capacity-building activities and of efforts to integrate environment within government. Through the initiative of ECG members, environmental units have been set up in all main departments and ministries. Before the NCS, only one department — Soil Conservation and Watershed Management — had an environmental division. Now, every sector is aware of the importance of environmental considerations in its planning and project cycle. The ECG has mobilized and consolidated support for the NCS process within government, and acted as the principal engine for policy reform appropriate to local conditions.

The NCS Implementation Project currently includes five programmes in the fields of environmental assessment, environmental planning, heritage conservation, education and public information.

Environmental Assessment

National guidelines for environmental impact assessment (EIA) were developed by the ECG and endorsed by cabinet in 1991. Sectoral EIA guidelines for industry, forestry and water resources have been drafted and are being tested by the relevant departments. EIA guidelines for other sectors are planned.

A national survey of industrial sources of pollution was conducted in 1990–91. Detailed assessment and management options are being prepared for high-priority problem areas and industries. The survey and management planning processes provide a comprehensive understanding of the country's industrial pollution problems, with enough quantified data to establish practical pollution standards and the technical capacity to apply them. A demonstration project has begun in one industrial area, and a pollution control management plan

has been prepared for another. This work has been guided by an inter-sectoral technical committee chaired by the NPC.

Another technical committee, involving government and NGO representatives, oversaw a comprehensive review of existing environmental law and administration. The review made detailed recommendations for institutional and legislative reforms and led to the redrafting of an umbrella environmental protection act and comprehensive regulations, including detailed provision for EIA procedures.

Environmental Planning

The ECG had formulated a national system of policies and standards for environmental planning. Following an extensive process of consultation and debate, the draft environmental legislation has incorporated a framework for planning at national and local levels. The NPC has facilitated the preparation and implementation of eight model village environmental plans in two districts. More village plans are underway; two district plans and one regional model environmental plan may also be prepared. They allow the environmental planning guidelines and draft legislation to be field-tested, particularly their underlying principles of local control and devolution of resource management responsibilities.

Heritage Conservation

The NCS Secretariat is working with the Nepal Heritage Society, other local NGOs and relevant government ministries to establish a process of registration and management of national heritage sites. The ECG has been involved in training and field activities to define and test the process of participatory heritage management, which also has been reflected in the draft environment legislation. A demonstration National Heritage Conservation Project has been initiated, covering the natural and built environment of the Panauti area near Kathmandu.

Environmental Education

This programme aims to enhance environmental management and resource conservation coverage in the formal and informal curricula of existing education and training institutions. The priority is environmental education in primary schools and has involved preparation of a model environmental curriculum, revision and expansion of current textbooks and development of resource materials. Institutions to train extension workers and government officers are also supported, and associated training materials prepared and tested.

These activities are being carried out with the Ministry of Education and Culture, Tribhuvan University, the Nepal

Administration Staff College, government training centres, the Institutes of Forestry and Agriculture and Animal Science, Women Development Programmes and several NGOs.

Other activities include regular national environmental education conferences, environmental camps for conservation awareness, and environmental art workshops and competitions for school children.

Public Information

Publications include an NCS newsletter, published regularly and circulated to over 1300 people, and publications related to implementation. Public awareness includes community-level wall newspapers, a weekly radio programme and a resource centre focusing on environmental issues of concern to Nepal. Some of these projects are implemented through local NGOs.

A nationwide network of journalists, trained through a series of media workshops, is preparing individual and group reports on environmental topics for the local and national media. A programme of street theatre has begun to help village communities understand and discuss key environmental issues.

Apart from these programmed implementation activities, the NCS team is regularly called upon to contribute to the range of additional environment initiatives that come before government. The NCS Secretariat, for example, was closely involved in preparing the documentation for UNCED. In 1993, the secretariat also helped prepare a National Environment Policy and Action Plan (NEPAP) at the behest of the World Bank. After initial resistance, the NPC adopted NEPAP as a logical review and revision of the NCS and a natural phase in the strategy cycle.

Technical studies

To address recent environmental degradation problems, technical studies are being carried out, including a 25-year Kathmandu Valley Perspective Plan.

6 Lessons Learned

The lack of continuity between phases of the NCS, with major gaps in 1984 and in 1987–88, slowed progress and required support to be rebuilt after each fallow period. This problem could have been avoided if some elements of strategy implementation had begun while government was considering policy options.

Strategy documents like Nepal's, which include a detailed Action Agenda, quickly become out-of-date, particularly in times of political change. This means that:

- the time spent on document preparation alone (rather than in combination with implementation) should be minimized;
- action plans that go into too much detail prior to implementation can take the sense of ownership and creative design away from implementing groups and communities;
- the NCS document (ie policy framework and action plan) should be regularly reviewed and updated to have the maximum impact on the conventional development planning cycle; and
- aspects of implementation should begin at the start of the NCS process in conjunction with document preparation.

Building capacity and awareness should start immediately, to increase political support for the process. In Nepal, earlier formation of the ECG could have helped generate support for the NCS, and widened the base of support. It could have ensured continuity between phases and addressed some of the inter-ministerial rivalries. The core group could also have been involved in environmental awareness and education from the start and helped set priorities.

Once established, the core group approach facilitated the development of a working network of committed technical officials who have the basic skills and familiarity with the new environment methods and policies to ensure that they are practised and sustained in government.

The status of the NCS as a project within government, but independent of it in terms of funding and staffing, has had advantages during the political upheavals and subsequent institutional adjustments that have shaken Nepal from the late 1980s to 1992.

NCS implementation project staff can concentrate on their work without being distracted by the day-to-day problems that crop up in a government department. This relative autonomy facilitated contacts with other ministries, which did not feel threatened by the NCS project as they might by another agency. The secretariat has also been able to act as a broker between government departments and aid agencies in negotiations over environmental activities. In addition, project status allowed specialist staff to be recruited both from within and outside government. This helped ensure that the secretariat had staff with the skills needed.

In the short term, the project approach has meant that NCS activities are undertaken quickly and effectively. Yet, as a project, the NCS team had to be acutely conscious of setting targets for the integration of each implementation

programme activity within government; in this, the role of the ECG was especially important.

The ties to the government's central planning body were essential in giving formal access to all sectors, in the credibility it brought to the NCS process, and in the direct access it gave to cabinet and the Prime Minister. Most important, the NPC is mandated to review and coordinate the annual and five-year development programmes of all governmental agencies. This process left a great deal to be desired in terms of effectiveness, but it placed the NCS at the hub of the government's policy and resource allocation process. The administrative and legal systems to take advantage of this position are being put in place slowly but steadily.

A key lesson of the Nepal NCS relates to the role of law and lawyers. Legislation is the culmination of a sometimes lengthy policy development and testing process, in which local lawyers should be involved. An understanding of new environment management methods, such as EIA, and of the options for legal expression, comes through working closely on their development in inter-disciplinary teams. Legislative drafting should not lag too far behind the definition of new approaches, but certainly should not proceed without building the necessary awareness and capacities in the lawyers concerned.

IUCN's role in providing consistent technical help and stimulation has been very important. This has been provided through local expertise, one permanent expatriate advisor and irregular input from IUCN's international expert networks. IUCN's bond with Nepal stems from the country's longstanding state membership in the union, going back more than 20 years. It ensured that the NCS always had strong institutional support, even when government was distracted and administrative links with the strategy process became blurred. The long-term commitment by the Swiss to funding the NCS process was crucial in maintaining IUCN's involvement.

The main weakness in the NCS process has been the lack of a united and coordinated approach to all elements of strategy implementation by donors and within government. The select range of activities addressed by the NCS implementation project as essential ingredients of an environmental administrative system were well coordinated and supported. Mechanisms for giving practical effect to the NCS as the strategic framework for all development investment and actions were lacking, however.

One reason was that, with delays in official endorsement, the NCS document lost its immediacy and relevance. The cycle of regular review and revision was not in place to keep the document current and fully engaged in the system. Competing sectoral plans, promoted through substantial grants by the Asian Development Bank and World Bank without sensitivity to the need to protect and nurture the NCS process, also made it very difficult for the NPC to maintain control. Finally, donor coordination in the environment field in general was weak. The government had no mechanism in place for the purpose. Its slow approach to developing environmental regulatory measures has created delays in implementation and has made the whole process less effective. UNDP attempted to establish an environment coordinating group, but institutional rivalries and imperatives, particularly involving the World Bank, sank the initiative. IUCN's potentially important role, as an independent technical organization helping government effectively assert its coordinating function, was limited by a lack of resources.

There needs to be a much more concerted effort by donors to broaden the base of support for the NCS in the long term and to do so in a way that reinforces the central core of activities and institutional initiatives managed through the NPC.

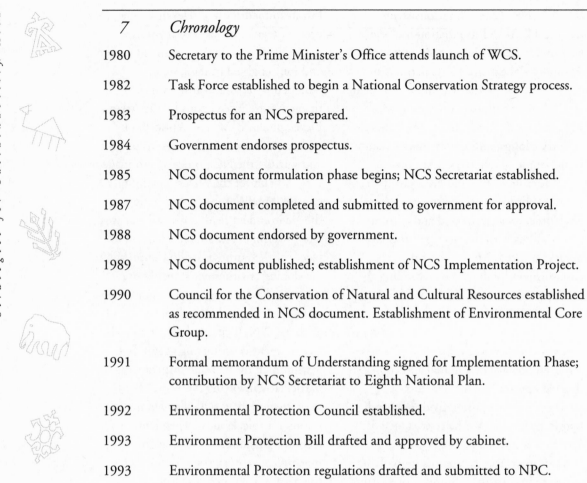

7 *Chronology*

1980	Secretary to the Prime Minister's Office attends launch of WCS.
1982	Task Force established to begin a National Conservation Strategy process.
1983	Prospectus for an NCS prepared.
1984	Government endorses prospectus.
1985	NCS document formulation phase begins; NCS Secretariat established.
1987	NCS document completed and submitted to government for approval.
1988	NCS document endorsed by government.
1989	NCS document published; establishment of NCS Implementation Project.
1990	Council for the Conservation of Natural and Cultural Resources established as recommended in NCS document. Establishment of Environmental Core Group.
1991	Formal memorandum of Understanding signed for Implementation Phase; contribution by NCS Secretariat to Eighth National Plan.
1992	Environmental Protection Council established.
1993	Environment Protection Bill drafted and approved by cabinet.
1993	Environmental Protection regulations drafted and submitted to NPC.

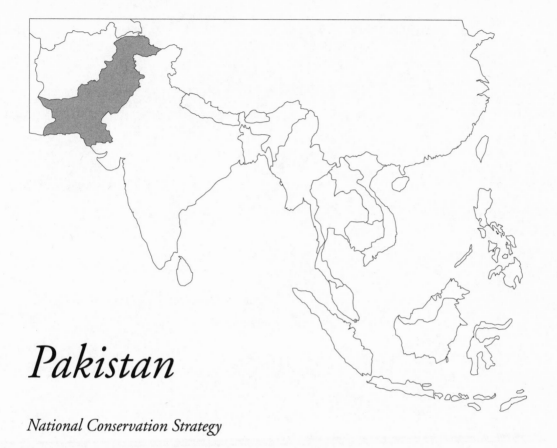

Pakistan

National Conservation Strategy

ABAN MARKER KABRAJI, G M KHATTAK AND SYED AYUB QUTUB

Population: 115.8 million; **Land area:** 796 000 square kilometres; **Ecological zones:** floodplain of river Indus, mountainous area, plateau, low-lying plains and desert in south; **Climate:** dominated by Asiatic monsoon, mountains cool in summer, snow in winter, upland plateau hot summers and cool dry winters; **Annual rainfall:** 150–1000 mm; **Forest area:** 25 000 square kilometres; **GNP per capita:** US$ 400; **Main industry:** agriculture, cotton, food processing, engineering; **ODA received per capita:** US$ 10.6; **Population growth rate:** 1991–2000, 2.8 per cent; **Life expectancy:** 59 years; **Adult illiteracy:** 65 per cent; **Access to safe water:** 50 per cent; **Access to health care:** 85 per cent; **Access to sanitation:** 22 per cent

1 Introduction and Summary

The Pakistan National Conservation Strategy (NCS) began with a two-year start-up phase, followed by three years of preparation, during which time a strategy document was prepared, reviewed, revised and submitted for cabinet approval. The NCS document was approved in 1992. The main implementation phase was launched with a donors' conference in January 1993, although some implementation began in 1991, with allocations in the federal budgets for 1991–92 and 1992–93. The implementation plan emphasized institutional strengthening and capacity-building and recognized that, although the strategic design must not be buried under a pile of individual projects, projects are important, because they are the most visible evidence of implementation. The strategy is now being extended into the provinces, with the development of provincial conservation strategies. In 1992 work began on the first of these: the Sarhad Provincial Conservation Strategy in the North West Frontier Province.

The Pakistan experience shows the necessity of having a strategy with an organization that will move it forward and keep it on track through changes in government and other vicissitudes. The Pakistan NCS also shows the value of high-level support for the strategy process from the national government; but indicates that such support is no guarantee that working levels of government will be fully involved. Participation in the strategy now needs to be increased both within and outside government.

2 Scope and Objectives

The NCS is a strategy to conserve the environment of Pakistan, maintain its resource base, and ensure that its development efforts are environmentally sound.

The strategy document describes 'where we are, where we should be, and how to get there'. In the first section, it assesses the state of Pakistan's environment, including land, freshwater and marine environments and resources, biodiversity, minerals, energy supply and demand, and cultural heritage. It reviews governmental, non-governmental and community institutions and organizations concerned with environment and development. It also analyzes the environmental implications of Pakistan's economic structure and policies, sectoral policies, and laws.

In the second section, the document proposes elements of a strategy covering; agriculture, forest management, rangeland rehabilitation, livestock management, water resources, marine and coastal resource management, fisheries, wildlife and their ecosystems, mineral resources, energy, industrial development, human settlements, pollution control, and recreation and tourism. It outlines supporting policies and measures on population, education, communications, research and technology, women in development, training, and environmental information systems.

Finally, the third part of the document sets out a ten-year action agenda and implementation plan. This identifies 14 core programmes:

- maintaining soils in croplands;
- increasing irrigation efficiency;
- protecting watersheds;
- supporting forestry and plantations;
- restoring rangelands and improving livestock;
- protecting water bodies and sustaining fisheries;
- conserving biodiversity;
- increasing energy efficiency;
- developing and deploying renewables;
- preventing and abating pollution;
- managing urban wastes;
- supporting institutions for common resources;
- integrating population and environment programmes; and
- preserving the country's cultural heritage.

For each of these programmes, the document specifies long-term goals, expected outputs by 2001, inputs to 2001, and critical tasks for the federal and provincial leadership, government departments, districts, communities, individuals, businesses, and NGOs. It also shows how to integrate these programmes into existing and proposed national, sectoral and subsidiary plans. The document then proposes building institutions to support the action agenda and implementation plan, paying particular attention to federal-provincial leadership, increasing inter-agency cooperation, enhancing departmental capacities, improving district-level coordination, involving the corporate sector, and cooperation with communities and NGOs. Finally, it outlines a plan for financing the strategy.

Aims of the NCS

The aims of the NCS are:

- to introduce fundamental changes in work and lifestyles to protect the interests of present and future generations;
- to facilitate the integration of environmental considerations into the daily economic, social and physical decisions of individuals, communities, companies and government;

- to facilitate the incorporation of environmental policy considerations into government's economic, social and physical development processes;
- to facilitate the environmental awareness-building roles of NGOs, to obtain early proclamations of environmental objectives and to promote the formulation of and adherence to environmental standards;
- to harness the energy of the private sector to support environmentally sensitive processes and products; and
- to revitalize community-based management for the sustainable use of common resources and infrastructure.

Objectives of the NCS

The NCS objectives are defined according to conservation, sustainable development and efficiency.

Conservation of natural resources:

- to maintain essential ecological processes;
- to preserve the biodiversity of natural resources; and
- to restore degraded natural resources cost-effectively.

Sustainable development:

- to ensure the sustainable use of natural resources;

- to extract exhaustible resources at rates that do not exceed the creation of substitute capital resources; and
- to ensure balanced and diversified development that maintains, if it does not increase, the options available to future generations.

Improved efficiency:

- to improve the efficiency with which natural resources are used and managed, raising their yields to their sustainable potential;
- to improve the way that associated resources and capital (ie community infrastruture) are used and managed;
- to give priority to conserving and improving best soils and sweet water; and
- to give priority to preventing deterioration of fragile ecosystems and large downsteam effects.

Operating Principles of the NCS

Principles governing the NCS process relate to public participation, integrating environment and economics, and quality of life.

Greater public participation in development and environmental management:

- to achieve better public awareness of environmental concerns;

- to encourage public participation and commitment to solve environmental problems;
- to communicate NGO concerns to government, and systems for adequate response; and
- to promote permanence in public participation by strengthening grassroots institutions.

A merger of environment and economics in decision-making by:

- allocating environmental responsibility to economic decision-makers; and
- installing environmental monitoring systems.

Durable improvements to the quality of life by:

- balancing natural resources and population;
- supporting durable improvements in the quality of human settlements;
- controlling and preventing pollution; and
- giving preference to biological solutions.

3 Relationship to Development Planning

Macro-economic and development planning are carried out in Pakistan by the Federal Planning Commission, which reports to the National Economic Council. Five-year plans embody the main development objectives, as well as programmes and projects. Subsequently, the planning commission also scrutinizes and approves all public sector projects above a certain magnitude.

The NCS Steering Committee was directly linked to the development planning system through its Chair, who, as Deputy-Chair of the planning commission, was the most senior civil servant on the development side, with the rank of a federal cabinet Minister of State. However, there was little everyday contact with middle-level officials in the planning commission.

Constituent programmes of the implementation plan have been incorporated in the Eighth Five-year Plan, which also includes a chapter on environment, based on the NCS document. As the document recommended, an environment section has been established in the Planning and Development Division within the Ministry of Planning to provide environment–economic policy analysis, and to integrate environmental considerations into planning, review large projects for environmental sustainability, and promote sustainable development projects. This is expected to further ensure the integration of NCS programmes into existing planning and decision-making.

4 Strategy Development

In December 1983, the Inspector-General of Forests, Ministry of Food, Agriculture and Cooperatives asked IUCN for a national conservation strategy. IUCN responded with a short mission in February 1984, which prepared a document outlining the rationale and scope of an NCS, a rough budget, and the necessary organizational arrangements. Two years elapsed while IUCN sought funding and discussed with the Government of Pakistan (GOP) which ministry should take the lead in developing the strategy. Eventually, GOP decided that the responsible federal agency should be the Environment and Urban Affairs Division (EUAD), rather than Food, Agriculture and Cooperatives, which was the original proponent, or the Planning and Development Division, which was recommended by IUCN.

IUCN proposed that a prospectus be prepared, the funding for which it obtained from CIDA. The prospectus and 12 sectoral papers were discussed in a national workshop sponsored by EUAD and IUCN in 1986. The workshop was attended by some 50 national experts, who reached a consensus that the country's environmental problems were serious and rapidly getting worse, and that they needed to be addressed in an cross-sector manner. The proceedings of the workshop were jointly published in 1987 (GOP, IUCN and CIDA: *Towards a National Conservation Strategy for Pakistan: Proceedings of the Pakistan workshop*. Asian Art Press, Lahore).

In 1988, the GOP commissioned IUCN to develop the NCS. A memorandum of understanding between EUAD and IUCN outlined the extent and cost of technical services and project equipment to be provided by IUCN, and indicated the basis of exemptions from duties and taxation on imported goods. CIDA provided IUCN with about CA$1 million for the NCS secretariat, commissioning of sector papers, workshops, public hearings, village meetings, and a journalist resource centre as the communication arm of the NCS. IUCN hired a Canadian and a Pakistani as joint coordinators of the NCS Secretariat. They started work later that year.

At this stage, the composition of the NCS steering committee still had not been decided. IUCN felt that it was critical for the strategy to be strongly linked with the planning system. It therefore requested and obtained the agreement of the Deputy Chair of the Planning Commission to head the steering committee. The Secretary of EUAD, responsible for environmental protection policy and programmes, was the Deputy Chair of the Steering Committee. The other members were the Secretaries (civil service heads) for Economic Affairs, Agriculture, Agriculture Research, Industries, Water and Power, Petroleum and Natural Resources, two corporate heads, a media leader, an advertising company chief executive, and the chief of Pakistan's largest NGO programme. Given this composition, the steering committee was seen to be a prestigious body and played a key role in the successful development of the NCS.

The NCS secretariat was housed in the EUAD, which then was a small, marginalized department in a not-very-powerful Ministry of Housing and Works. The secretariat reported to the Chair of the Steering Committee for all technical and substantive matters. It reported to IUCN HQ, and later to the IUCN Country Representative in Pakistan, for administrative matters. The secretariat worked closely with EUAD to ensure consistency with current or proposed environmental protection plans.

The division of reporting led to a certain amount of tension between the secretariat and IUCN-Pakistan. However, the existence of a government-based steering committee and secretariat on the one hand and a politically astute and locally-based international NGO on the other meant that the strategy was pushed ahead by two engines rather than one.

The NCS secretariat was responsible for preparing the strategy. The coordinators devised a two-year work plan and set of guiding principles. They discussed them with the Chair of the Steering Committee, who drew up the list of sectors to be included in the cross-sectoral analysis. A search proforma was prepared for experts in these sectors. Each potential author was visited, and 18 were identified, along with three or four peer reviewers each. Authors were called together for an authors' conference in October 1988, and given generic terms of reference requiring papers that focused on interactions among sectors.

Preparation of the strategy document took three years. More than 3000 agencies and individuals were consulted, including schools and colleges in Islamabad, Karachi and Lahore. Among the few interests whose direct involvement could not be obtained were the military and religious constituencies, artists and literati, small industry and labour unions, and rural local governments.

Review of information, consideration of options, and reaching agreement involved:

- provincial and sectoral workshops to review draft sector papers and generate options (inconsistencies between sector reports were sent to all the authors concerned for comments and reconciliation);

- drafting sub-committees to correct sectoral recommendations and policy options;
- comments on first, second, and third drafts of the NCS document from all divisions of federal government and all four provincial governments;

- public hearings and village meetings;
- ten meetings of the steering committee to consider principles, workplans, options, drafts, and to review and approve the NCS document; and
- defining targets and costing in the third draft in consultation with sectoral experts and other key policy advisers.

Chart D: Participants in the Pakistan NCS Process

Interests	Involvement	Level
federal govt.	steering committee, authors, provincial workshops, review by all 48 divisions, drafting sub-committees, review of final draft	all
provincial govt.	provincial workshops, peer reviewers, drafting sub-committees	middle
autonomous bodies	authors, provincial workshops, drafting sub-committees	senior
local (urban)	provincial workshops	middle
corporations	steering committee	heads
environment NGOs	provincial workshops, sectoral workshops	heads
population NGOs	authors, sectoral workshops	senior
development NGOs	steering committee, sectoral workshops, peer reviewers	heads
universities	public hearings	senior
research institutes	authors, provincial workshops, sectoral workshops	senior
media	steering committee, provincial workshops, sectoral workshops	leaders
women	steering committee, provincial workshops, sectoral workshops, village meetings	leaders/ individuals
farmers	village meetings	individuals
communities	village meetings	individuals
concerned citizens	village meetings, bulletin	individuals

Agreement in the steering committee and the drafting sub-committees was generally by consensus. Sometimes this entailed bypassing difficult issues, especially to avoid loss of face by an agency. It also led to the deletion of a major focus on social equity issues.

The draft NCS document was approved by the steering committee in July 1991. The NCS was approved in a special one-agenda session of cabinet in March 1992, where it was presented with graphics and a film by the Additional Secretary of EUAD and the Minister, and supported by a number of ministers who had been actively lobbied by IUCN and EUAD before the meeting.

IUCN-Pakistan played a key role in facilitating the strategy both within and outside government, as did CIDA, which, as the principal source of funds, contributed some CA$3 million. UNDP played a supporting role in funding sector workshops. Apart from the joint coordinator, who resigned after 18 months, expatriate consultants were used only for specific short-term tasks. Most of the work was done by Pakistanis, ensuring that the strategy was locally relevant.

Under its contract with IUCN, CIDA retained responsibility for monitoring and evaluating the strategy's preparation. A Canadian consultant undertook four monitoring missions during this phase,

and facilitated a participatory evaluation by associated individuals in November 1991. This evaluation was culturally foreign to Pakistani participants, who were not used to discussing their views openly and on an equal basis with colleagues, especially their superiors. Nonetheless, it revealed some interesting insights. Participants considered the NCS to be an excellent technical and policy framework for sustainable development in Pakistan, but noted several areas where it could have been improved, including:

- inadequate emphasis on equity and poverty, the basic needs of the majority of people, the informal economy, and population;
- a heavy focus on central government, no doubt due to the fact that the federal government commissioned the NCS and the fact that federal government membership on the steering committee outweighed business and NGO membership — (although the consultation process included provincial workshops, there was little involvement of provincial governments);
- little substantive community participation or involvement of business and industry, due to limitations of staff and resources; and
- insufficient involvement of EUAD staff and other departments in development of the NCS, partly because the secretariat did not have time to run a full-scale outreach programme, even

within the federal government, while preparing drafts.

5 Implementation and Results

The action plan in the NCS document is not specific enough to serve as an implementation programme. In August 1991, therefore, following completion of the document, IUCN conducted nine implementation design workshops, involving research, federal, provincial, education and training, judicial, urban, business, communications, and community development institutions and constituencies. This extended participation in the strategy to many who knew little about the content of the NCS document, and these sectors have continued to be involved in sector-specific programmes.

When cabinet approved the strategy, it set up an NCS Implementation Committee, headed by the Minister of Environment, and including other key ministers (Finance, Agriculture, Education, etc). Under this committee's direction, the NCS Unit and an IUCN consultant jointly drafted an implementation plan for a donors' conference held in January 1993. The GOP document presented to the conference was based on this plan. The implementation committee approved an action plan with four components:

- strengthening technical, regulatory and planning institutions, local participatory institutions, and private sector institutions (this focused on an NCS unit in EUAD to coordinate the NCS, provincial conservation strategy units to coordinate at the regional level, an environment section in the Planning Commission, improving federal and provincial environmental protection agencies, strengthening technical institutions, establishing environment cells in chambers of commerce and industry, strengthening NGOs, and returning responsibility for primary schools, basic health units and local natural resource management to local government);
- formulating a coherent broad-based communications campaign for mass environmental awareness (capacity-building for this began early in the preparation phase with the establishment of the Journalists' Resource Centre of IUCN);
- creating a supportive framework of regulations and economic incentives (this focused on the adoption of an Environment Protection Act, development of sector-specific economic incentives to promote conservation of the environment and natural resources and to combine economic and environmental sustainability); and

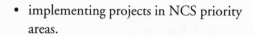

- implementing projects in NCS priority areas.

The first three components demonstrate a clear emphasis on capacity-building as well as a recognition that the strategic design must not be buried under a pile of individual projects. The projects are important, however, because they are the most concrete and visible evidence of NCS implementation. The action plan stresses the need for this visibility and for the three other components to be directly and visibly linked to the projects.

To focus implementation and provide the best impact for the project component, the fourteen core programmes of the strategy document have been reduced to eight:

- increasing irrigation efficiency;
- protecting watersheds;
- restoring rangelands and improving livestock;
- protecting water bodies and sustaining fisheries;
- conserving biodiversity;
- increasing energy efficiency;
- preventing and abating pollution; and
- managing urban wastes.

One or two projects in each of these programmes will be given priority as high-profile projects to demonstrate the concrete results of NCS implementation to the public. The projects are divided

into three benefit categories: enhancing human welfare, increasing economic efficiency, and promoting nature conservation.

The budget for implementation has been reduced from US$600 million per year of additional investments to a more realistic US$100 million per year over the five year period of the Eighth Plan, or about 0.5 per cent of the gross domestic product. The NCS document proposed that 59 per cent of the required resources come from the corporate sector, but the sector was not consulted adequately for a programme into which it was supposed to have such a large input.

At an implementation conference in January 1993, the donor community responded positively to the general principles and concepts of the NCS and the government's NCS Plan of Action. However, donors were not exactly sure what steps to take in supporting full-scale NCS implementation. In addition, they were concerned about expensive commitments in times of budget restraint, and expenditures in areas where there were already high donor commitments and low rates of disbursement due to the low absorptive capacity of the Government of Pakistan.

Responding collectively to these concerns, the Multi-Donor Coordination Group for NCS Implementation subsequently appointed a Donor Technical Working Group (DTG). The DTG consisted of seven technical advisors from CIDA, UNDP, the UN Food and Agricultural Organisation (FAO), GTZ, and IUCN. The working group was charged with making specific recommendations to donors on immediate steps that they could take to support the NCS.

This proved to be a critical component that had been overlooked in the initial implementation plans for the NCS. It involved clearly showing to government and donors how to get from the status quo to the plan laid out in the NCS. The DTG identified areas in support of the NCS in which there were few or no investments, along with areas where existing donor commitment should be refocused to better meet NCS objectives. The donor community and the Government of Pakistan now have a realistic plan for phased and cost-efficient implementation of the NCS.

The institutional capacity to implement the strategy is being developed by establishing an NCS unit in EUAD and an environment section in the Planning and Development Division. Both are staffed by GOP personnel and funded in part by donors. IUCN continues to maintain an NCS support unit. The donor base has been diversified to include the Norwegian, Swiss, Dutch and British aid agencies. The NCS secretariat was disbanded on completion of the strategy document, leaving no NCS component within government for 18 months until the NCS unit was set up in EUAD. However, the Additional Secretary in the Ministry of Environment took on the work of shepherding the document through the cabinet approval process; and the ministry also processed approval for establishment of the NCS Unit.

Among other results of the NCS so far are:

- an Environmental Protection Act is being drawn up;
- the Supreme Court has created special environmental appeal procedures to accommodate public interest litigation, which some of the smaller NGOs have taken up with success;
- round tables have been established to involve the corporate sector;
- increased participation by women (a women's NGO has started a programme on women and the environment, and the Forestry Institute is providing a training course for women in forestry development);
- training is being provided in environmental assessment; and
- a Sustainable Development Policy Institute has been set up.

The NCS is being extended into the provinces through the development of provincial conservation strategies. An environment section, which has as its

65

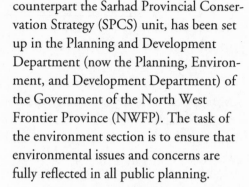

counterpart the Sarhad Provincial Conservation Strategy (SPCS) unit, has been set up in the Planning and Development Department (now the Planning, Environment, and Development Department) of the Government of the North West Frontier Province (NWFP). The task of the environment section is to ensure that environmental issues and concerns are fully reflected in all public planning.

The SPCS is being developed with the approval of the Chief Minister, and is overseen by a steering committee chaired by the Additional Chief Secretary, who heads the Planning, Environment, and Development Department (the central planning unit at the provincial level). Steering committee members include secretaries and heads of government departments, politicians, and representatives of NGOs, the media, the Chamber of Commerce, and industries. IUCN is providing technical assistance, including the coordinator. Work on the SPCS began in 1992 to do the following:

- identify high-priority areas for NWFP out of the recommendations of the NCS;
- interpret NCS recommendations in the light of the conditions of NWFP;
- obtain additional information on priority environmental concerns to facilitate their amelioration; and
- promote action programmes to address those concerns.

A monitoring and evaluation procedure for the NCS is being developed.

6 Lessons Learned

Factors Favouring the Strategy

Factors favouring the strategy during start-up were:

- EUAD had an able Joint Secretary in 1986;
- the national workshop (August 1986) helped build up consensus;
- the financial support of CIDA;
- credibility provided by the World Conservation Strategy and the Brundtland Commission Report; and
- IUCN's knowledge of the political system.

During preparation the strategy benefitted from:

- the high-level, cross-sectoral steering committee, and exceptionally able leadership of its Chair;
- a capable Pakistani coordinator;
- CIDA's flexibility in accommodating an evolving process; and
- IUCN-Pakistan's strong technical support.

Factors favouring approval of the strategy include:

- the quality of the document and the consensus-building process that led to it;
- the support of key departments, EUAD and the Planning and Development Division; and
- the political networking of the IUCN country representative (IUCN-Pakistan left nothing to chance, providing the presentation to cabinet and rehearsing it with the secretary and minister).

The key factors favouring full-scale implementation were:

- creation of the cabinet implementation committee immediately after approval;
- drafting of the implementation plan for the donor conference; and
- the broad constituency of support for the NCS as a result of the process of consultation.

Factors Hindering the Strategy

Factors hindering the strategy during start-up were:

- a delay in donor funding between start-up and preparation; and
- the failure to secure an institutional home in the Planning and Development Division.

Obstacles during preparation were:

- the departure of the expatriate coordinator in mid-stream and inability of short-term replacements to complete their tasks due to other commitments or unavoidable problems (this was overcome through extra hard work by national staff);
- the inability of short-term consultants and non-specialists to understand the intricacies and nuances of the sectors addressed by the strategy (this was overcome by working with drafting sub-committees of sectoral experts representing all interests); and
- weak integration with working levels of government.

Factors hindering implementation were:

- departure of the head of NCS unit for the World Bank;
- ministerial rivalry over preparation of the implementation document; and
- delays in the donors' conference, risking a loss of momentum and of the overall sense of strategy in the implementation document through ad hoc initiation of miscellaneous projects.

Remaining Obstacles and Problems

There are still considerable obstacles. The NCS has set a course but the strategy needs to be widened to extend beyond the federal government to provincial and local governments, businesses, NGOs and communities. It also needs to be deepened, involving more people in each of these groups, rather than just the leaders and a sampling of others.

The strategy has made great progress, but compared with the scope of the issues it addresses, it is still only a beginning. Further institutional development is needed, together with continuing and expanded political will, additional human and financial resources, greater and more widespread environmental awareness, and attention to social equity. Remaining problems include lack of education, entrenchment of vested interest, and a lack of good governance and its conse-quence for democratic norms essential to further strategy development.

Few people have read the NCS document. The concepts, messages and technical information still need to be communi-cated widely and effectively.

The relatively broad-based steering committee for preparation was replaced by a cabinet committee of federal govern-ment. The advantage of this is that decisions have the force of cabinet. However, a coalition outside government is needed to take actions that government will not take, together with mechanisms to link and coordinate governmental and non-governmental actions.

Main Lessons

The entire strategy must be placed in the heart of the economic planning process of government. It must not only be a part of central planning, it must be seen to be taken seriously by the most powerful and important ministries within the govern-ment system and have their sustained involvement and backing.

The successful implementation of a strategy depends as much on the process of its development as on the technical competence of the strategy document. A coalition of key interests needs to be developed for the strategy. Participation by these people in preparation of the strategy document is essential for them to feel that the strategy is theirs and to take responsibility for its implementation. Where an interest group is expected to take up a substantial share of the implementation, as was the case with the corporate sector, the group should be closely involved in deciding the content of the implementation plan.

The strategy has benefitted from two engines to drive it forward and keep it on track. One was the steering committee and NCS secretariat; the other was IUCN-Pakistan. Although the dual reporting lines of the NCS secretariat caused tension, the combination of forces within and outside government proved highly effective in getting the strategy document completed and adopted. Great care is needed, however, to ensure that the groups work closely together and do not diverge. Much of the work of increasing government participation in the strategy now falls to the NCS Unit, which will need strong and consistent support.

Communicating the strategy, its process and its messages are a key to its success. This requires a team of professionals who understand its conceptual basis and dynamics, as much as its technical content. Although a fairly sophisticated communication programme existed, the NCS team realized that specialized formal and informal communication skills are needed to reach communities and other potential participants.

Donors and other external supporters of the strategy need to be kept well-briefed on the strategy process, so that when the time comes for financial support for implementation, they understand the concept and are ready to respond.

Strategies must walk before they can run. If they take on too much, in terms of subject scope or participation, they run the risk of getting bogged down or fragmented. The NCS has been criticized for its inadequate emphasis on equity and poverty, the basic needs of the majority of people, the informal economy, and population. Yet the NCS document was probably already somewhat over-ambitious in scope, and its implementation plan has had to be scaled down to more practical dimensions. Clearly, strategies cannot cover everything, and if they try to do so they will not be strategic. It is better for the first cycle of the strategy to set a clear and strong direction and be somewhat modest in scope, increasing the issues it addresses in later cycles as progress is made.

Similarly, the strategy has been criticized for concentrating on the federal government without fully involving departmental staff, and for insufficient involvement of provincial governments, communities, and the corporate sector. Yet the wide consultation conducted by the NCS secretariat stretched its resources and could not have been expanded. Clearly, greater participation is needed, but this too can be achieved through successive cycles of the strategy.

7   *Chronology*

1983   December: Inspector General of Forests, Ministry of Food, Agriculture and Cooperatives asks IUCN for a National Conservation Strategy.

1984   February: IUCN mission prepares *First Steps*, outlining the rationale for and scope of an NCS, providing a rough budget, and describing institutional arrangements needed.

1986   March–April: IUCN consultant funded by CIDA prepares an NCS prospectus.

1986   August: GOP (EUAD)/IUCN-sponsored National Workshop discusses prospectus and 12 sectoral papers, and calls for an NCS.

1987   Workshop proceedings, *Towards a National Conservation Strategy* published jointly by GOP, IUCN and CIDA.

1988   January: CIDA funds IUCN.

1988   April: GOP/IUCN memorandum of understanding. Technical Secretariat established.

1988   May: Steering Committee notified.

1988   June: objectives, principles, work plan, outline format of strategy, and search proforma for authors approved at First Steering Committee meeting.

1988   October: Authors Conference.

1988   November–December: Draft sector papers (18 sector authors).

1989   December–January: Four provincial workshops; 200 participants review draft papers and develop options.

1989   January: Ten policy and programme papers and a sector paper on heritage conservation commissioned (NCS Secretariat).

1989   February 1989–February 1991: Revised sector and prescriptive papers, comprising 5000 pages, 29 authors.

1989	April–June: draft Chapters 1 and 2 of NCS approved by Steering Committee and circulated to all 48 federal divisions, 4 provinces, paper authors (NCS Secretariat).
1989	October: draft Chapters 3 and 4 of envisaged 6-chapter strategy completed and approved by Steering Committee for circulation.
1989	October: IUCN advisor leaves over dispute with IUCN regarding the administrative role of IUCN-Pakistan.
1989	November: IUCN recruits short- term periodic consultants to help finalize the strategy.
1989	November 1989–June 1990: Comments on drafts received, NCS chapters 1–4 revised, work plan revised.
1990	March–April: Village meetings and public hearings (NCS Secretariat/IUCN country staff).
1990	January–April: Completion of first draft Chapters 5 and 6; Implementation Arrangements and Communications.
1990	March: CIDA approves extension for one year.
1990	April–May: Sector Workshops (NCS Secretariat/IUCN staff).
1990	May: Steering Committee wants more specific implementation arrangements, but draft approved for circulation.
1990	June: Revised 13-chapter format, separating State of Environment (SOE), Issues and Opportunities, and Implementation Arrangements.
1990	July: Steering Committee Chairman approves revised format.
1990	August 1990–March 1991: Drafting and revision of 13 NCS chapters by NCS Secretariat, IUCN advisors and consultants through close consultation with and direction from the Steering Committee and its Drafting Sub-Committees, comprising federal, provincial and independent experts.
1991	July: Steering Committee approves NCS document.

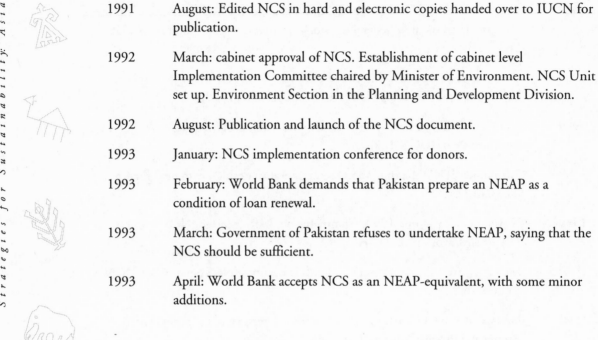

1991   August: Edited NCS in hard and electronic copies handed over to IUCN for publication.

1992   March: cabinet approval of NCS. Establishment of cabinet level Implementation Committee chaired by Minister of Environment. NCS Unit set up. Environment Section in the Planning and Development Division.

1992   August: Publication and launch of the NCS document.

1993   January: NCS implementation conference for donors.

1993   February: World Bank demands that Pakistan prepare an NEAP as a condition of loan renewal.

1993   March: Government of Pakistan refuses to undertake NEAP, saying that the NCS should be sufficient.

1993   April: World Bank accepts NCS as an NEAP-equivalent, with some minor additions.

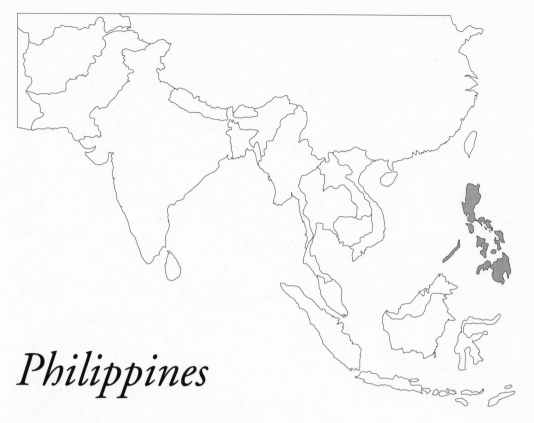

Philippines

Strategy for Sustainable Development

DULCE M CACHA

Population: 62.9 million; **Land area:** 300 000 square kilometres; **Ecological zones:** largely mountainous, narrow coastal margin and broad interior plateau; **Climate:** humid and tropical in lowlands; **Annual rainfall:** 2080 mm at Manila; **Forest area:** 95 000 square kilometres; **GNP per capita:** US$ 730; **Main industry:** agriculture, lumber, oil, copper; **ODA received per capita:** US$ 16.7; **Population growth rate:** 1.9 per cent; **Life expectancy:** 65 years; **Adult illiteracy:** 10 per cent; **Access to safe water:** 81 per cent; **Access to sanitation:** 70 per cent

1 Introduction and Summary

The Philippine strategy for sustainability is embodied in two documents: the Philippine Strategy for Sustainable Development (PSSD) and the Philippine Agenda 21. Adopted by cabinet in 1989, the PSSD defines goals, objectives, and guiding principles; and includes situation reports, key issues, current efforts and key sectoral measures. The Philippine Agenda 21, adopted in September 1992, is the national blueprint for action on sustainable development from now to the 21st century. It is based mainly on the PSSD, the Philippine National Report to UNCED, and UNCED's Agenda 21.

The PSSD was preceded in 1983 by an NGO-produced NCS document, which had little impact. Government began work on a national conservation strategy in 1987, renaming it as a sustainable development strategy following the publication of *Our Common Future*. The PSSD became the corporate strategic plan for the Department of Environment and Natural Resources (DENR); was incorporated in the master plan of the Department of Agriculture; and has been used to justify funding projects. It has not otherwise been implemented.

Philippine Agenda 21 is intended to be integrated into the Philippine Medium-Term Development Plan (1993–1998)

and has the potential to be a potent force for sustainable development. Appropriately, the Philippines Council for Sustainable Development, established by government to turn Philippine Agenda 21 into action, is chaired by the National Economic Development Authority (NEDA). However, the secretariat for Agenda 21 has been assigned to the agricultural staff of NEDA, which risks sidelining Agenda 21 as a sectoral, rather than national, endeavour.

2 Scope and Objectives

The PSSD document covers population, environment and natural resources (forests, protected areas and biodiversity, urban ecosystems, freshwater ecosystems, coastal resources, land and mineral resources), agriculture, industry, and energy. Its goal is 'to achieve economic growth with adequate protection of the country's biological resources and its diversity, vital ecosystem functions, and overall environmental quality'.

Objectives of the PSSD

PSSD objectives are:

- to ensure the sustainable utilization of the country's natural resources, such as forests, crop lands, marine and freshwater ecosystems;

- to promote social and inter-generational equity in the utilization of the country's natural resources;
- to develop management programs to preserve the country's heritage of biological diversity;
- to promote the technologies of sustainable lowland agriculture and upland agro-forestry through research and development and demonstration projects;
- to achieve and maintain an acceptable quality of air and water;
- to promote research and development in environmentally sound and economically efficient processing of the country's mineral and energy resources;
- to enhance the foundation for scientific decision-making through the promotion and support of education and research in ecosystems;
- to promote and support the integration of population concern through migration variables and family welfare considerations in development programmes, with special emphasis on ecologically critical areas; and
- to substantially expand the family planning programs and responsible parenthood programs.

At the core of the strategy are a number of implementing devices, including:

- integration of environmental considerations in decision-making;

- proper pricing of natural resources;
- property rights reform;
- establishment of an integrated protected areas system;
- rehabilitation of degraded ecosystems;
- pollution control;
- integration of population concerns and social welfare in development planning;
- inducing growth in rural areas;
- promotion of environmental education; and
- strengthening citizens' participation and constituency building.

The *Report on Philippine Environment and Development: Issues and Strategies* (UNCED National Report. 1991. Bureau for Environment Management, Department of Environment and Natural Resources, Manila) presents a history of economic growth and environmental management efforts in the country, and discusses development planning and the way the environment has been considered in it. Detailed discussion of the major sectors cover development trends and environmental issues and concerns. Major sectors considered in the report are forestry, minerals, agriculture, protected areas and biodiversity, coastal and marine resources, energy, industry, urban ecosystems, and special concerns such as natural disasters, indigenous communities, and the role of women in environment and development.

The report also reviews several issues identified as challenges for sustainable development, including debt relief; poverty and population; resource destruction; rapid urbanization; natural disasters and environmental degradation; lack of access to environmentally-sound technology; climate change; and hazardous wastes.

The report presents the PSSD's goals, objectives, guiding principles and strategies, related activities and additional measures and recommendations. It includes a proposed Philippine Action Plan on Sustainable Development for the period 1993–2002. The plan is organized by sector, indicating key issues, existing legislation and activities, proposed strategies, the institutions involved, and a timetable for the short term (1992–95), medium term (1992–97), and long term (1992–2002).

The Philippine Agenda 21 consists of numerous activities and recommendations corresponding to most of the programme areas of UNCED's Agenda 21.

3 Relationship to Development Planning

The PSSD and Philippine Agenda 21 are explicitly tied in to the development planning system, but have not yet been integrated with it.

Due to limited time after development of the PSSD conceptual framework, projects included in the draft action plan were mostly those of DENR. Consequently, they focused more on environment and natural resources than on sustainable development. Existing and proposed policies and projects of the major sectors were simply categorized to fall within the conceptual framework. There was no attempt to analyze the policies and projects and discontinue or redesign those which were inconsistent with the objectives and principles of the PSSD. Thus the PSSD has not been integrated into the planning and decision-making processes of any of the major sectors.

The Philippine National Report noted that '...despite the passage of Cabinet Resolution No. 37, mandating the line agencies to integrate the PSSD into their plans, programs and budgets, the pacing and rate of adoption by such agencies leaves much room for improvement. While DENR has achieved vertical coordination on environmental matters extending from the national to the regional and local levels of government, horizontal coordination (or the actual integration and coordination of environ-mental-related programs) between the DENR and other environmental-related agencies as well as within the agencies themselves have been minimal. What is needed is effective follow-through actions by the DENR as the PSSD coordinating agency, and the NEDA as the national economic planning body, in order to ensure that other agencies would translate the PSSD into specific agency action and budget plans/programs/projects'.

Alternatively, the national report recommends consideration of a new arrangement whereby NEDA sponsors the PSSD and adopts this as a major development strategy in the updated Philippine Medium-Term Development Plan (MTDP). This would entail reorientation of the whole development plan to embody the PSSD as an integral part.

An order in support of the executive order adopting the Philippine Agenda 21 directs that it should be integrated into the updated MTDPs (1993-1998) of local government units. The MTDP was scheduled to be completed by the end of 1992. The order also directs the Department of Interior and Local Government (DILG) to ensure that Philippine Agenda 21 and the goals and objectives of the PSSD are integrated into the plans, programmes and projects of all local government units. The DILG, in coordination with the DENR, NEDA and other concerned government agencies, was also directed to disseminate PSSD and Philippine Agenda 21 to personnel in local government units and help them prepare their own local Agenda 21. However, problems with coordination of implementation (*see section 5*) cast doubts on this integration.

4 Strategy Development

Philippine National Conservation Strategy

In response to the World Conservation Strategy, the Haribon Society, a Philippine-based NGO (now named The Haribon Foundation), prepared a national conservation strategy document. The Philippine Presidential Committee for the Conservation of the Tamaraw, plus individuals and organizations from government, business, academia and NGOs, also participated in its preparation. USAID provided financial support through a fund administered by the Asia Foundation. The NCS document was published in 1983. Its proposals were not implemented and the document was forgotten with the other programmes of the Marcos regime following the revolution in 1985.

Philippine Strategy for Sustainable Development

In 1987, the Environmental Management Bureau (EMB) was formed within the DENR. One of its functions was 'to coordinate the inter-agency committees that may be created for the preparation of the State of the Philippine Environment Report and the National Conservation Program'. Accordingly, the EMB initiated preparation of a national conservation strategy. In 1988 the strategy was renamed the PSSD to reflect its full scope.

The PSSD is meant to be expressed by three documents: a conceptual framework, policy and institutional reform measures, and an action programme. However, only the conceptual framework has been adopted and published. The policy and institutional reform component has not been completed, although a number of proposed policy reforms have been approved. An action plan has been drafted and copies given to foreign donors, but it has not been published or incorporated in the plans, programmes and budgets of government agencies.

Preparation of the conceptual framework included a national workshop and a symposium involving participants from government, academia, NGOs and industry. These were followed by a series of multi-sectoral regional consultations and briefings on the draft document. After each consultation, EMB revised the draft to incorporate comments, presenting a revised draft to the next consultation. Periodic DENR management conferences were used by the EMB to present the draft to DENR regional executives. A draft was reviewed in early 1989 by a senior officials' consultative forum, attended by high-level decision-makers from the executive and legislative branches of the government, academia, business, international agencies and NGOs. The draft conceptual framework then made its way through various cabinet subcommit-

tees, before being adopted by cabinet, with some modification, in November 1989.

Growing concern for the environment by many sectors and interests in the Philippines generated a lot of comments on the draft PSSD. Consultations were rather selective, however, and there was no systematic attempt to consult with all the groups concerned.

No additional staff were assigned to the development of the PSSD, and staff who worked on it did so in addition to their other functions. The costs of preparation and consultation were met from EMB's regular budget, except for the senior officials' consultative forum, which was supported by UNDP.

Philippine Agenda 21

In 1991, President Aquino set up a National Coordinating Committee (NCC) to prepare for the participation of the Philippines in UNCED. The Secretary of Foreign Affairs was the Chair, with 12 cabinet secretaries and a representative of environmental NGOs as members. A national technical committee of senior officials was established to support the NCC. DENR was the lead agency for the preparation of the Philippine National Report. A draft was written by a core group of experts, and reviewed first by

EMB and then by regional and national multi-sector consultations.

The adoption of Agenda 21 by UNCED committed the participating governments to redirect their national plans and programmes on environment and development. The first response by the Philippines was the workshop 'Response to the Earth Summit: Implementing the Philippine Agenda 21 for Sustainable Development' held from 31 August to 1 September 1992 by the EMB, DENR, NEDA, UNDP, CIDA and the Philippine Futuristic Society (an NGO). During the workshop, high-level representatives from the government, NGOs, experts, and the international donor community validated the Philippine Agenda 21, the Philippine Action Program on Sustainable Development (based on the PSSD), the Philippine National Report, Agenda 21, and additional input from concerned agencies and groups.

The culmination of the workshop was the signing of an executive order by President Ramos establishing a Philippine Council for Sustainable Development (PCSD). The mandate of the PCSD is to provide the mechanism for attaining the principles of sustainable development and assure their integration in national policies, plans and programmes involving all sectors of Philippine society.

During the 60-day transition period after the signing of the executive order, a technical working group formulated operational guidelines for the PCSD. Hereafter, the PCSD is expected to operate regularly with the support of a secretariat based at NEDA, the central economic policy and planning agency in the Philippines. Much of the technical support is expected to be provided by DENR.

However, coordinating and overseeing implementation of the strategy has been assigned to the agricultural staff of the NEDA, effectively relegating it to a sectoral concern rather than making it an overall national sustainable development strategy. Also, although NEDA chairs the PCSD, it has stated that it is in no position to implement the strategy. It has since arranged with DENR for the latter to provide the required technical and support.

5 Implementation and Results

Between adoption of the conceptual framework in 1989 and UNCED preparation in 1991, implementation of the PSSD was limited to its presentation to donors and the Department of Budget and Management as the framework for DENR's programmes and projects. In 1992, the Department of Agriculture adapted the PSSD conceptual framework and incorporated it in its master plan. External funding of projects required presenting potential donors with comprehensive documents on natural resources and environmental planning: preferably an adopted framework or strategy. Accordingly, the PSSD became the justification for many of the projects and programmes funded by foreign and international organizations from 1990 on. Some of these are:

- The USAID natural resources accounting project. The first phase covered forest resources; the next phase will cover mineral resources.
- The World Bank's Environment and Natural Resources Sectoral Adjustment Loan (SECAL). This includes a regional resources management programme; a monitoring and enforcement project; and an integrated protected areas system project. The first phase of this project was completed in 1992, and included passage of the National Integrated Protected Areas System Act, identification and study of ten priority sites and training of DENR and NGO personnel. The next phase will cover the protection and management of the sites. This is the main biodiversity conservation programme in the Philippines.
- The USAID Natural Resources Management Program (NRMP), assisting economically and ecologically sus-

tainable forest resource management and the protection of biodiversity within old-growth forests. The programme provides support for policy reforms in the areas of land tenure, forest charges, entry into and exit from the forest products industry, privatization of government holdings, old-growth forest protection, residual forest management, technology development and transfer, community-based forest management, and monitoring and evaluation. The programme makes use of a debt-for-nature swap to establish an endowment fund that will support NGO activities on biodiversity conservation.

- The Asian Development Bank's support for development of a National Master Plan for Forests. The plan has been completed and draft regional master plans have been prepared.
- The Energy Sector Program, supported by the International Bank of Reconstruction and Development (IBRD), which aims to strengthen DENR Regional Offices and the EMB through provision of training and modern laboratory facilities. It also aims to establish baseline sampling stations for air quality and to enhance capabilities to assess, manage and monitor the environmental impact of energy projects.
- The UNDP-supported project on Human Resources in Environmental Planning and Management for Sustain-

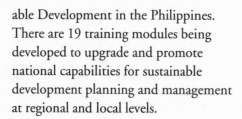

able Development in the Philippines. There are 19 training modules being developed to upgrade and promote national capabilities for sustainable development planning and management at regional and local levels.

While the rationale for these programmes can be found in the conceptual framework of the PSSD, they were developed independently of each other. There was no conscious effort to integrate the PSSD in their design or formulation. As a result, there are gaps and duplication. Conditions attached to grants or loans stimulated or accelerated several policy reforms. Some were real hurdles for the Government of the Philippines to overcome, notably forest charges and the National Integrated Protected Areas System (NIPAS) law and its implementing rules and regulations.

Procedures for monitoring and evaluating implementation of the strategy are unclear. DENR is required to formulate and enforce a system of measuring and evaluating its performance periodically and objectively and to submit the results to the President of the Philippines annually. Funding organizations also require monitoring and evaluation of projects. However, such monitoring and evaluation is not within the context of the PSSD, which in any case has made no provision for them.

6 Lessons Learned

Formulation of the Philippine strategy was motivated by a combination of events: growing environmental awareness, sharpened by disasters such as the eruption of Mount Pinatubo; the publication of *Caring for the Earth* and *Our Common Future*; and UNCED. Yet although these events stimulated the preparation of documents, they were not enough to foster an appreciation within government of the need for a strategy, for integration of environment and development, or for sustainable development.

The PSSD and Philippine Agenda 21 documents were prepared quickly, but this speed may have resulted in a superficial understanding of them. Evidently, the strongest stimulus to action has been provided by conditions attached to loans and donations. However, the donors and lenders have used the PSSD simply as evidence that a framework document had been adopted and a particular condition had been met. They have not used the PSSD as a strategy that should shape and coordinate their support.

This suggests a need to root the strategy more deeply both in government development and planning agencies and in the international donor community by greater participation of the former and thorough briefing of the latter.

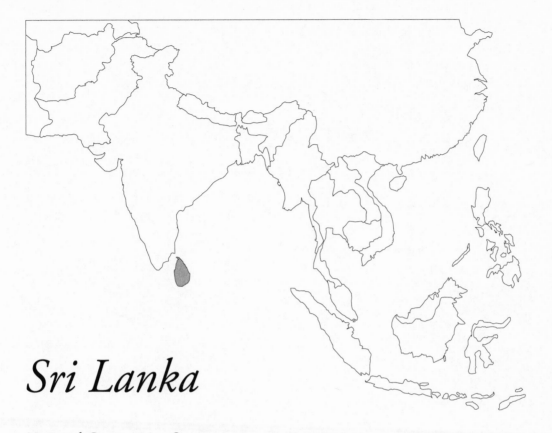

Sri Lanka

National Conservation Strategy

M S RANATUNGA, LESLIE C A WIJESINGHE AND RANJIT A WIJEWANSA

Population: 17.2 million; **Land area:** 66 000 square kilometres; **Ecological zones:** tropical monsoon forest, open woodland, arid northern region; **Climate:** high temperatures and humidity in north, greatest rainfall on southwest coast and in mountains; **Annual rainfall:** 1626–5537 mm; **Forest area:** 17 000 square kilometres; **GNP per capita:** US$ 500; **Main industry:** agriculture, timber, fishing, graphite; **ODA received per capita:** US$ 47.5; **Population growth rate:** 1.1 per cent; **Life expectancy:** 71 years; **Adult illiteracy:** 12 per cent; **Access to safe water:** 60 per cent; **Access to health care:** 90 per cent; **Access to sanitation:** 50 per cent

1 Introduction

To date, Sri Lanka's strategy process has been dominated by the preparation of documents. An NCS document was completed in 1988. It was followed in 1990 by a Draft Action Plan setting out a large number of activities to implement the NCS. After World Bank intervention, an Environmental Action Plan was prepared in 1991 to identify high priority actions. The government felt that this was too narrowly focused, and prepared an NEAP for the period 1992–1996, which Cabinet approved in 1991.

At the same time, a comprehensive document (USAID 1991. *Natural Resources of Sri Lanka: Conditions and trends.* USAID, Washington, D.C.), set out quantitative data on current trends in resource use and their impact on the environment.

The Sri Lanka National Report to UNCED, published in 1991, describes the links between environment and development. It is expected that the UNCED report and the NEAP will serve as the blueprint for environment and development programmes in Sri Lanka.

2 Scope and Objectives

The major objective of the NCS is to ensure that environmental protection is incorporated into the development strategy of the country.

The NCS document is divided into six parts:

- environmental profile;
- management of ecosystems for sustainable development;
- human activities involving the environment;
- constraints to environment conservation and sustainable development;
- the strategy policy; and
- implementation.

The NEAP is the programme of action for implementing the NCS. It identifies 12 programme areas:

- land resources;
- water resources;
- mineral resources;
- coastal resources;
- forestry;
- biodiversity and wildlife;
- urban pollution;
- industrial pollution;
- energy;
- environmental education;
- culture; and
- institutional capacity.

For each programme area there is a broad overview followed by sections on the key issues to be addressed. The current state of the issue is outlined, followed by a series of recommendations, priorities, costs, and recommended implementing agencies. Implementing agencies are interpreted broadly to include government, NGOs and the private sector.

3 Relationship to Development Planning

Because the NEAP includes an investment plan, it is closely linked with the Department of National Planning in the Ministry of Policy Planning and Implementation. This ministry is responsible for the rolling five-year plan, including the Public Investment Programme (PIP). The PIP outlines planned public investments by sector. Government departments and ministries submit annual plans to the Department of National Planning, which matches resources to priority programme areas. The 1990 PIP states that 'environmental concerns and conservation measures are...treated as integral components in the development effort'.

4 Strategy Development

The government first showed interest in an NCS following consultation with IUCN in 1977. Strategy development began in 1982 when the President of Sri Lanka appointed a task force to prepare the NCS as Sri Lanka's response to the World Conservation Strategy. The task

force was headed by the Chair of the Central Environment Authority.

Preparation of the NCS document took six years. Two workshops were held: one in 1984 to draft guidelines for the preparation of sector papers; the other in 1986 to review progress and to draft the format for the NCS document. USAID provided financial support for the two workshops and for the services of three consultants.

The task force commissioned sectoral papers on 27 subjects; there were no papers on cross-sectoral links. Papers took several years to complete; some authors left their posts and new specialists joined the project. The task force met regularly, but members were high-level public officials with heavy demands on their time. This, together with a lack of resources and guidance from senior officials, contributed to delays in preparing the document.

In 1988, the National Environment Act was revised to give control and regulatory functions to the Central Environment Authority (CEA). That same year, following the release of the NCS document, the CEA prepared a Draft Action Plan (DAP). A steering committee was established under the Chair of the CEA to oversee the process. Key issues from the NCS document were classified into six sectors, and a working group was appointed for each sector. Working group members were specialists who had been involved in preparing the NCS. Ministries, departments, corporations, universities and NGOs were consulted. The working groups prepared a document outlining the issues, actions and key implementing agencies. Workshops and informal meetings were held to discuss and revise the DAP, which was published in November 1990.

Also in 1990, the World Bank and the newly-established Ministry of Environment and Parliamentary Affairs (MEPA) prepared an Environmental Action Plan (EAP). A small group of specialists was selected to draft a document that would highlight the priority areas for action. The EAP drew heavily from the DAP; but the government considered it too narrowly focused.

In 1991, therefore, MEPA prepared an NEAP. Cabinet approved the NEAP that year, and regards it as the definitive national action plan for the environment for the period 1992–1996. The Ministry of Environment is responsible for catalyzing and coordinating implementation.

5 Implementation and Results

Since the preparation of one strategy document was followed by the preparation of another, there has been little systematic implementation. However, there have been a number of indirect results.

Government adoption of the NCS and the NEAP are signs of its commitment to developing a practical national environmental strategy linked to the economic development and planning system. Additional evidence of the improved political climate for addressing environmental issues includes the creation of the Cabinet Committee on Environment, the strengthening of the National Environment Act, and the establishment of a National Environmental Steering Committee (NESC). NESC is responsible for monitoring and evaluating the progress of the NEAP. It consists of representatives of different ministries and is co-chaired by the Secretaries of the Ministry of Policy and Planning and Implementation and the Ministry of Environment and Parliamentary Affairs. However, due to staff shortages, it has not been very active.

6 Lessons Learned

The succession of strategy documents from 1982 to 1991 culminated in a more focused definition of what needed to be done; each document was an improvement over its predecessor in this respect. Nonetheless, it seems likely that results would have come more quickly if greater

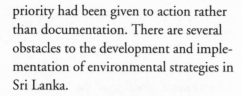

priority had been given to action rather than documentation. There are several obstacles to the development and implementation of environmental strategies in Sri Lanka.

Inadequate Financial Resources

The Government of Sri Lanka finds it increasingly difficult to finance the priority actions set out in the NEAP. A high level of donor support is necessary to implement the recommended actions and programmes. Donor-funded projects have time constraints, with little or no capacity to sustain local staff once a project is complete. Unless government takes over the staff, the capacity that has been build up during the project is lost. But government usually lacks the resources to assume these costs. Also, the more a strategy relies on donors for funding, the more likely it is to break up into unrelated projects and lose strategic coherence.

Inadequate Capacity

There is a serious shortage of trained personnel, particularly at the professional level in MEPA and the CEA. In other ministries and departments, staff are barely able to fulfill the minimum requirements of their jobs, let alone take on new responsibilities relating to the environment. Also, there is little capacity within

the private sector to handle environmental matters such as pollution abatement and EIA.

Institutional Weaknesses

The main institutional weaknesses identified in the NEAP are:

- lack of clear institutional mandates and responsibilities for environmental policy-making at the national level;
- fragmentation and lack of coordination among the many agencies with responsibilities for land, water or other natural resource management; and
- lack of capacity for pollution control and monitoring.

Conflict with Development

The government's economic development programme envisages a sharp growth in industrialization. This will mean more conflicts between environment and development. This has not been sufficiently addressed in the environmental strategy documents to date, largely because the they have not been prepared as part of economic and development policies. One of MEPA's priorities is to extend the NEAP into an Agenda 21: a national plan of action to encourage develop priorities while addressing environmental issues.

7 Chronology

1977   Initial interest shown by Sri Lanka in an NCS following discussions with IUCN.

1982   Sri Lanka decides to prepare an NCS as its response to the WCS. Task force appointed by the President to guide NCS preparations.

1983   Workshop held to draft guidelines for sector papers.

1983–87   27 sectoral technical papers prepared.

1986   Workshop held to review progress and to draft format for NCS document.

1988   NCS document completed. National Environment Act (NEA) revised.

1990   Regulations for pollution control under the NEA gazetted. DAP prepared.

1991   Sri Lanka Natural Resources Profile prepared identifying trends in resource use. NEAP prepared. UNCED National Report. NEAP and National Report approved by Cabinet and passed to the Ministry of Environment and Parliamentary Affairs for implementation.

Glossary

Agenda 21	Statement of principles and action plan for sustainable development, from the 1992 Earth Summit in Rio
BARC	Bangladesh Agricultural Research Council
CEA	Central Environment Authority (Sri Lanka)
CESP	Commission on Environmental Strategy and Planning (IUCN)
DANIDA	Danish International Development Agency
DENR	Department of the Environment and Natural Resources
DEPC	Department of Environmental Pollution Control (Bangladesh)
DILG	Department of the Interior and Local Government (The Philippines)
DTG	Donor Technical Group (Pakistan)
EAP	Environmental Action Plan
ECG	Environmental Core Group (Nepal)
EIA	Environmental Impact Assessment
EMB	Environmental Management Bureau (Philippines)
EPC	Environment Protection Council (Nepal)
EPU	Economic Planning Unit (Malaysia)
EUAD	Environment and Urban Affairs Division (Pakistan)
FAO	Food and Agricultural Organization (UN)
GOP	Government of Pakistan
GTZ	Deutsche Gelleschaft für Technische Zusammenarbeit
IBRD	International Bank of Reconstruction and Development
IIED	International Institute for Environment and Development
IMF	International Monetary Fund
IUCN	The World Conservation Union
MEPA	Ministry of Environment and Parliamentary Affairs (Sri Lanka)

MOEF	Ministry of Environment and Forests (Bangladesh)	NWFP	North West Frontier Province (Pakistan)
MOU	Memorandum of Understanding	PCSD	Philippine Council for Sustainable Development
MSTE	Ministry of Science, Technology and Environment	PIP	Public Investment Programme (Sri Lanka)
MTDP	Medium-Term Development Plan	PSSD	Philippine Strategy for Sustainable Development
NCC	National Coordinating Committee (The Philippines)	SIDA	Swedish International Development Agency
NCS	National Conservation Strategy	SOE	State of Environment
NEAP	National Environmental Action Plan	SPCS	Sarhad Provincial Conservation Strategy
NEDA	National Economic Development Authority (The Philippines)	UNCED	United Nations Conference on Environment and Development
NEMAP	National Environment Management Action Plan	UNDP	United Nations Development Programme
NES	National Environmental Strategy	UNEP	United Nations Environment Programme
NGO	Non-governmental organization	UNSO	United Nations Sudano-Sahelian Office
NORAD	Norwegian Agency for International Development	USAID	United States Agency for International Development
NPC	National Planning Council (Nepal)	WCS	World Conservation Strategy
		WRI	World Resources Institute
		WWF-M	Worldwide Fund for Nature, Malaysia